*Critical Guides to French Texts*

94  Corneille: Rodogune *and* Nicomède

*Critical Guides to French Texts*

EDITED BY ROGER LITTLE, WOLFGANG VAN EMDEN, DAVID WILLIAMS

# CORNEILLE

# Rodogune *and* Nicomède

**Derek A. Watts**

Reader in Classical French Literature
University of Exeter

**Grant & Cutler Ltd**
**1992**

© Grant & Cutler Ltd 1992

ISBN 0 7293 0346 2

I.S.B.N. 84-599-3297-4

DEPÓSITO LEGAL: V. 3.591-1992          6 0 0 3 7 5 5 5 7 x

Printed in Spain by
Artes Gráficas Soler, S.A., Valencia
for
GRANT & CUTLER LTD
55-57 GREAT MARLBOROUGH STREET, LONDON W1V 2AY

# Contents

## Prefatory Note

All quotations from the text of the two plays, and all line references, are taken from the Nouveaux Classiques Larousse editions of *Rodogune* (*5*) and *Nicomède* (*8*), both published in 1975. All modern editions in fact are based on the text of 1682, and the differences between them are negligible apart from spelling and punctuation, which have been modernised except in *3*. (All such italicised numbers refer to the numbered items in the Bibliography at the end of this volume. Other figures in brackets are line-references to the text of each play.)

# Introduction

Why link these two plays together? To begin with the most practical reason, they are the only tragedies by Pierre Corneille, outside the 'famous four' (also known as 'the tetralogy'), to have maintained over three centuries a foothold on the French stage.[1] As a result, they figure more regularly in the academic syllabus than do other works by the same author that the professional theatre has consigned to virtual oblivion. Their contrasting yet in many ways complementary features reveal most of the qualities and themes that have ensured Corneille's fame. As for theatrical qualities, *Rodogune* might be described as the author's principal showpiece, and *Nicomède* as his most accomplished piece of stagecraft. Each play is dominated by an evil oriental queen who tries to perpetuate her own power by exploiting, and if necessary by destroying, her own or her husband's offspring. In *Rodogune* Corneille gives a striking display, not only of near-melodramatic stage effects, but also of resounding rhetoric, whereas *Nicomède* discards the grandiloquence in favour of quick-fire repartee, cogent argument and swift action. Neither work presents a profound moral conflict, yet at the heart of each one is an implicit statement on the nature of *vertu* and *générosité*. Both plays are political tragedies centred on the lust for power, but it is in *Nicomède* rather than *Rodogune* that we find problems and ideas worthy, in Corneille's day at least, of serious debate.

---

[1] According to statistics published in a special number of *Europe* devoted to Corneille (540-41, April-May 1974), *Rodogune* and *Nicomède* ranked sixth and seventh respectively among Corneille's plays in the repertoire of the Comédie Française between 1680 and 1973, with 461 and 392 performances, well behind *Le Cid* (1567), *Horace* (887), *Le Menteur* (835), *Cinna* (768) and *Polyeucte* (708). *Nicomède* was in the billing for the Salle Richelieu in 1988-89.

In chronological order, *Rodogune* (first performed during the winter of 1644-45) and *Nicomède* (early 1651) are respectively the eighth and thirteenth of Corneille's serious plays. They therefore belong to the middle period of his long and prolific theatrical career (1629-74), a phase during which his dramaturgy underwent a number of important changes. In the 'tetralogy' which spanned the years 1637-43, Corneille had perfected his own distinctive brand of heroic drama. Its essence was psychological and moral conflict, and his protagonists — Rodrigue in *Le Cid*, the eponymous heroes of *Horace* and *Polyeucte*, and the emperor Auguste in *Cinna* — achieved renown for their ability to endure and solve painful dilemmas. These involved a choice not between easily identifiable 'good' and 'evil', but between two causes which commanded equal respect: on the one hand fidelity in love, and on the other family honour (*Le Cid*), patriotic zeal (*Horace*), allegiance to a just ruler (*Cinna*) and religious faith (*Polyeucte*), or between justice and clemency (also in *Cinna*). In these four plays, Corneille achieved a unique kind of equilibrium — a perfect marriage between 'external' theatrical effectiveness and 'internal' psychological interest. He also solved most of the problems of stagecraft which resulted from the necessity to accommodate a genuinely dramatic plot within the framework of the newly-imposed three unities of time, place and action. There is a tragic dimension to these plays, in that heroic triumph can be achieved only through agonising conflict, but final victory always proves to be within the hero's grasp; what may at first have appeared as a cruel, relentless Fate is ultimately revealed as a benign Providence, of which the hero is the chosen instrument. These plays were nevertheless all subtitled *tragédie*, the tragicomedy *Le Cid* being re-labelled thus in 1648. The use of this term was determined not by an unhappy ending or by any particular qualities that we would now recognise as 'tragic', but rather by certain formal criteria: five acts, characters of elevated rank, a plot involving danger and weighty political issues, and uniform seriousness of diction and tone.

A long-established view, often challenged today, is that *Le Cid*, *Horace*, *Cinna* and *Polyeucte* collectively represent the summit

of their author's achievement, and offer a true and sufficient image
of his genius — one that is more difficult to recognise in his subsequent productions, beginning with *Pompée*, first performed towards
the end of 1643. What happened to Corneille the dramatist at this
point in time is an intriguing question. It involved some important
changes of subject-matter, viewpoint and technique. *Pompée* is the
first play to bear witness to the transformations that used to be
known as the 'decline' of Corneille. Now between the writing of
*Polyeucte* and that of *Pompée* occurred a notable event: the death of
the all-powerful Prime Minister Cardinal Richelieu (4 December
1642). It has been contended that this event was the direct cause of
Corneille's change of manner. Certainly the Cardinal's attempts to
reorganise the theatre, in the interest of French national prestige, and
also as a propaganda machine, appear to have given a sense of
purpose to a number of dramatists, including Corneille. Corneille's
dedication of *Horace* to Richelieu contains a fairly explicit declaration of allegiance, but his subsequent references to Richelieu after
the Cardinal's death are more ambivalent (*1*, I, p.1062), and it may
be more prudent to conclude that Richelieu's disappearance from the
political scene and the dramatist's apparent loss of 'heroic momen-
tum' were merely coincidental (*39*, p.23). The coincidence is
nonetheless remarkable.

Compared with the 'tetralogy', the ten plays which Corneille
wrote in the period from 1643 to the beginning of his first
'retirement' from the theatre are difficult to classify. They tend, however, to fall into pairs. There are two comedies, *Le Menteur*
(contemporaneous with *Pompée*) and *La Suite du Menteur* (1644-
45); two spectacular 'tragedies of intrigue', *Rodogune* (close in date
to *La Suite du Menteur*) and *Héraclius* (1646-47), to which might be
added a second martyr tragedy, *Théodore*, to form 'la trilogie des
monstres' (*13*, ch. vii); and two 'heroic dramas', namely *Don Sanche
d'Aragon* (1649-50), classified by its author as a *comédie héroïque*,
and *Nicomède* (early 1651), both characterised by bright optimism
and a certain panache. These qualities are shared to some extent by
the machine play *Andromède* (early 1650). On the other hand,
*Pertharite* (1651-52), perhaps Corneille's most enigmatic tragedy,

stands alone. Its failure was no doubt the prime cause of the author's six-year 'retirement' from the stage which began in 1652.

Difficult though these plays are to describe collectively, there is no doubt that in some respects Corneille seems to be turning his back on his previous achievement. In the first place, the admirable equilibrium between 'inner' and 'outer' content, characteristic of the tetralogy, is now abandoned, and as a result some of the less obvious features of the earlier plays now come to the fore. The plot itself gains greater prominence and hence greater complexity. The motives of the characters, and especially conflicts of motive within the characters, are now of less importance than the success or failure of their plans. In *Rodogune* and *Héraclius* especially, Corneille seeks to prove his skill as a 'technician' of plot-construction, by means of elaborate effects of mystery, suspense, surprise and symmetry. A problem of identity is sometimes involved; usually it is the legitimate ruler or heir to the throne whose identity has to be established. Violence and cruelty threaten to replace heroism as the dynamic force of the action. The more elementary types of political motive — ambition and vengeance — are developed at the expense of weightier political and moral considerations, which are rather thin on the ground between *Pompée* and *Nicomède*. The genuinely 'Machiavellian' doctrine expressed in *Horace* and *Cinna*, that the interests of the State must always prevail when the survival of that State is at risk, now becomes perverted and abused by unscrupulous rulers and their counsellors. The role of the hero is increasingly passive, and the male characters in some plays (especially *Rodogune*) tend to become overshadowed by virile and domineering women. Love continues to play a significant role, but more often as no more than an important piece on an essentially political chessboard, and it is becoming more and more influenced by romanesque conventions typical of contemporary fiction. Finally, the dramatist seems inclined, after *Pompée*, to look for his material in the obscurer by-ways of ancient history, no doubt in order to secure greater freedom of invention.

By 1652, therefore, Corneille had become a more complex and unpredictable dramatist than he had been ten years earlier. But in one vital respect, his genius remained unaltered: in his mastery of dramatic rhetoric. We find him equally at home in two contrasting styles of writing. On the one hand, there is majestic eloquence full of 'pompe' (to use a term which in Corneille's day was not derogatory) as in the great deliberation scene (II, 1) of *Cinna* or the first monologue of Cléopâtre in *Rodogune*. Abundant use of the standard rhetorical devices — in particular accumulation, repetition and antithesis — produces the almost mathematical balance of certain noted passages, in which perfect symmetry of language enhances the balanced presentation of ideas. On the other hand, the cut and thrust of lively dialogue is equally memorable in some other passages, such as Rodrigue's challenge to the Count in *Le Cid* (II, 2), or Nicomède's vigorous exchanges with Flaminius (III, 3).[2] In such contexts, Corneille makes use of two other devices of dramatic rhetoric: *sentences* or maxims, encapsulating a moral truth in (most often) a single alexandrine; and rapid exchanges of one-line sallies, in imitation of the 'stichomythia' of Greek tragedy. But the art of rhetoric, as widely taught in Corneille's day, did not consist solely of the manipulation of language: as well as *elocutio* there was *inventio*, that is the art of finding the most telling arguments, or the right descriptive details with which to fill out a narrative. Both as a pupil of the Jesuits, and also no doubt as a lawyer, Corneille had acquired these skills to a high degree, with the result that each of his characters is allowed to expound his or her case, even if it is a bad one — and there are plenty of those in our two plays — with the maximum dramatic impact. 'Arrêtez-vous où vous voudrez', wrote Diderot of Corneille, 'c'est toujours celui qui parle, qui semble avoir raison.' The ensuing pages will, I hope, provide ample opportunity to apply some of these general observations to the text of each play.

---

[2] This type of broken dialogue is more typical of *Le Cid* (in which the average length of the speeches is 5.1 lines) and of *Polyeucte* (4.6) than of *Horace* (9.1) or *Cinna* (8.2); but each play contains fine examples of each style of dramatic writing. There is a similar but less marked contrast between *Rodogune* (7.3) and *Nicomède* (5.4); if, however, we compared each play up to the end of Act III only, the figures would be: *Rodogune*, 9.2; *Nicomède*, 5.3.

# 1. Rodogune

## i) Rodogune in the Theatre

In the absence of reliable information, the date of the first performance of *Rodogune* can be fixed only by deduction and conjecture. It is usually placed in the winter of 1644-45 (*1*, II, pp.1268-69). The play's most striking feature, the predominance of two major feminine roles, has been attributed to the simultaneous presence, at that time, in Floridor's company at the Théâtre du Marais, of two star actresses, La Beaupré and Marie de Hornay (*23*, I, p.87). A variety of evidence suggests that *Rodogune* was an outstanding success. Firstly, there is the self-congratulatory tone of Corneille's dedication to the Prince de Condé, of the *Avertissement* of 1647 and the *Examen* of 1660. In addition, it was soon imitated by an author hired by the rival company at the Hôtel de Bourgogne. Gabriel Gilbert's tragi-comedy *Rhodogune* is an impudent plagiarism of Corneille for much of its first four acts, but Act V provides an improbable happy ending (see *3*, pp.117-31). Finally, there is the late date of the first edition, January 1647. Delay in publication usually indicated a box-office success, for in the absence of copyright protection, the rival troupes could preserve their monopoly only by withholding the text.

This initial success was long maintained. *Rodogune* was in the repertoire of the Hôtel de Bourgogne in 1678, as can be seen from a note in the final section of that invaluable document on seventeenth-century staging, the *Mémoire de Mahelot*. The décor and props used were minimal, but there is mention of the unusual requirement for Act V, namely 'trois fauteuils, un tabouret, une coupe d'or'. According to the *Registre de La Grange*, Molière's company performed *Rodogune* twenty-seven times in all. Throughout the eighteenth century, its popularity remained steady. During the first thirty-five years of the Comédie Française (1680-1715), it topped the bill among Corneille's fully-fledged tragedies, its total number of performances (134) being surpassed only by *Le Cid* (220) and *Le Menteur* (174). It was translated into English in 1765, and the censures of critics such as Voltaire and Lessing testify to its popularity. Its decline after 1820 was sudden and swift, and it is now only occasionally given at the Comédie Française, though one such revival in the 1960s achieved no less than twenty-five performances. So *Rodogune* has had a long and glorious career on the stage, having contributed to the reputation of performers such as Dumesnil, Gaussin, Clairon, Lekain, Talma, Georges, Dorval and Segond-Weber (*14*, pp.253-54).

## ii) A Bold Invention

*Rodogune* has constantly divided the critics. It is really a case of those who admire Corneille above all for his skill in plot invention, who are naturally enthusiastic, versus those who demand solid intellectual input, who are apt to be disappointed. There can be no doubt of Corneille's own view: it is implied in the *Avertissement* and proclaimed in the *Examen* and in the *Discours* of 1660. In the *Examen*, he is not far from claiming that *Rodogune* is his masterpiece:

> Cette tragédie me semble un peu plus à moi que celles qui l'ont précédée, à cause des incidents surprenants qui sont purement de mon invention, et n'avaient jamais été vus au théâtre; et peut-être enfin y a-t-il un peu de vrai mérite qui fait que cette inclination n'est pas tout à fait injuste. [...] Mes autres pièces ont peu d'avantages qui ne se rencontrent en celle-ci: elle a tout ensemble la beauté du sujet, la nouveauté des fictions, la force des vers, la facilité de l'expression, la solidité du raisonnement, la chaleur des passions, les tendresses de l'amour et de l'amitié et cet heureux assemblage est ménagé de sorte qu'elle s'élève d'acte en acte. (*5*, p.141)

Corneille's enthusiasm clearly stems from his view of *Rodogune* as a brilliant 'machine' for the production of theatrical emotion. Later on in the *Examen*, he makes this even more startlingly plain, when defending the character of Rodogune against the charge that her command given in Act III, Scene 4 is 'indigne d'une personne vertueuse'. Having explained all the morally extenuating circumstances, he suddenly abandons the ethical point of view and boldly declares:

> Je dirai plus: quand même cette proposition serait tout à fait condamnable en sa bouche, elle mériterait quelque grâce, et pour l'éclat que la nouveauté de l'invention a fait au théâtre, et pour l'embarras surprenant où elle jette les princes, et pour l'effet qu'elle produit dans le reste de la pièce qu'elle conduit à l'action historique. (5, p.145)

No other text by Corneille more clearly reveals his showman's love of the startling dramatic gambit, and no work more convincingly proves it than *Rodogune*.

These same texts reveal another reason for the pride Corneille took in this play. This was the dominating part played in its creation by original invention. More than any other tragedy of his, he saw *Rodogune* as his own brain-child, in which he had the audacity to 'feindre un sujet entier sous des noms véritables' (5, p.33). However, this does not deter him from attempting to impress his readers with the historical erudition on which his plot is based. He gives precise references to passages of Appian, Justin, I Maccabees and Josephus (5, pp.32, 35).

The use Corneille made of these sources was in fact quite limited. They provided him with a point of departure (the killing at Cleopatra's instigation of her faithless husband Demetrius Nicanor) and a point of arrival (her murder of her son Seleucus, and her death at the command of his brother Antiochus). Yet the intricate exposition of *Rodogune* includes a long succession of authentic historical details, many more than the audience really needs in order to grasp the basis of the plot. We learn in Scene 1 (26-69) that

Cléopâtre's husband had waged war on the Parthians, who took him prisoner; that, faced with Tryphon's rebellion, Cléopâtre had entrusted her two sons, Antiochus and Séleucus, to the care of her brother Ptolémée, King of Egypt; that Nicanor's brother (also called Antiochus) had become King of Syria after marrying Cléopâtre who believed her former husband to be dead; that after the defeat and death of Tryphon, Antiochus reigned seven years before embarking, like his brother before him, on a fateful campaign against the Parthians. Furthermore, in Scene 4 (216-63) we are told of Antiochus's eventual defeat and death in battle; of Nicanor's prosperity in captivity and of his marriage to the sister of the Parthian king, Rodogune; of his subsequent return with an army to reconquer Syria, and of his murder in an ambush, at Cléopâtre's instigation. These details are all vouched for by at least one ancient historian, as are the two events which constitute the play's dénouement: Cléopâtre's murder of Séleucus, and her own death in attempting to kill Antiochus.

Imagination provided all the rest. No historian mentions that Cleopatra's sons were twins and that she alone knew the order of their birth — a great *trouvaille* on the dramatist's part, for it needed a rare situation and an acute dynastic problem of this kind to provide the elements of rivalry and revenge, of symmetry, suspense and surprise with which the author sought to endow his plot. Another important invention was the amorous involvement between both of Nicanor's sons and his widow (who for reasons of *bienséance* is transformed into his ex-fiancée: the princes must not be allowed to woo their own step-mother!). The dramatist's final idea was to have Rodogune accompany her betrothed on his fateful expedition to Syria, and to have her captured and held hostage by Cléopâtre; this forces the Parthians to sign a truce, the terms of which are an important factor in the plot (264-88).

Never before had Corneille undertaken such a bold reshaping of history. In the *Avertissement*, he is already careful to distinguish between 'les effets de l'histoire' — major historical events that must be accurately represented in their essentials — and 'les circonstances' or 'les acheminements', which he claims lie within the dramatist's domain of invention — a distinction he later maintains in his

*Discours de la tragédie* (2, pp.46-47, 53). For some of the inventions in *Rodogune*, we can find parallels in Greek tragedy which may have directed Corneille's imagination along certain paths. The avenging of a father's murder upon the guilty mother is the basis of the Orestes-Electra-Clytemnestra story. In contrast, the close bond of affection between the twins Antiochus and Séleucus (192-210) recalls several examples of brotherly love in classical mythology, and notably that of the twins Castor and Pollux. Several lines in the play (particularly 171 ff.) suggest that Corneille was well aware of the mythological parallels, but he chose to direct his plot along strikingly different lines (*1*, II, pp.1278-81; *30*).

### iii) A Feat of Dramatic Engineering

*Rodogune* has been aptly described as a 'tragedy of intrigue': its main interest lies in its plot, which is developed using techniques we normally associate with comedy (*39*, p.18). For instance, information is divulged or withheld so as to produce effective combinations of suspense and surprise. The formal perfection of the plot also results from a careful *dosage* of symmetry and contrast. Each act after the first is centred on one major encounter (or, exceptionally, two) which is skilfully prepared and exploited. The events of Acts II and III follow an almost caricaturally similar sequence, but such is the fascination exerted by the dominant female personality — first Cléopâtre, then Rodogune — that comic perspectives are kept well out of sight. Only in Act V is there an uninterrupted crescendo movement towards the final scene, which with its use of props (the poisoned chalice) and the setting (the throne room) has come to be regarded as the 'showpiece spectacular' of seventeenth-century French tragedy.

The exposition, however, is a lumbering affair; in the *Examen* (*5*, pp.142-43), Corneille defends it as best he can. True, he has attempted to lighten the audience's burden by inserting two brisker scenes (I, 2-3) into Laonice's long narrative, but this affords only temporary relief. Nevertheless a lot can be said in favour of these early scenes. Suspense is gradually built up in preparation for the shocks of Act II. Laonice begins by stressing the solemnity of the day that is dawning, the day on which the Queen will reveal the identity of her successor. 'Mais n'admirez-vous point', she adds (15) — is Timagène not amazed? — that she is preparing to marry the lucky twin to her prisoner Rodogune, the object of her hatred? In order to *mieux admirer* (23), he asks to be up-dated, after his long absence in Egypt, on recent events in his homeland — a common pretext for a theatrical exposition. Laonice's account is, however, soon interrupted by the anxious Antiochus (Scene 2), who, in explaining his impatience, provides more 'key facts' for the audience. He has fallen in love with Rodogune, but he is also deeply attached to his brother; as a solution to this dilemma, he has decided to offer Séleucus the throne in exchange for the princess. He has scarcely time to entrust Timagène with this mission, when his brother arrives in person, in order to make an identical proposal on his own behalf. There is a strong hint of comedy in these paradoxically symmetrical events, and the ironical 'mirror effect' is enhanced by the patterned dialogue (134-38,143-50). Antiochus is now lucid enough to realise that their mutual plan is useless, for whoever marries Rodogune must have a throne to offer her. Séleucus concludes that an even greater effort of fraternal devotion is now required, for it is all or nothing for each of them (183-84). Mystery and suspense are intensified by the hint that Cléopâtre's word may not be as good as that of a mother and a queen ought to be. Having exchanged a pledge of mutual fidelity, the princes depart, leaving Laonice to complete her account of recent events (Scene 4). In reply to Timagène's enquiry, she declares her ignorance of her mistress's reaction to the princes' adoration; but this doubt is quickly dispelled by Rodogune's own confession in Scene 5 (355-70). However, she firmly declines to name the object of her love, and silences Laonice's attempt to guess (385).

Thus Act I ends with uncertainty surrounding the vital issues that will shape the plot. Rodogune's first utterances underline her reasons for distrusting Cléopâtre (299-327). Our curiosity is frustrated by her pledge never to reveal her heart's secret, for she intends to sacrifice her love to her duty to marry the heir to the

Syrian throne, whoever he may be. A triple question is thus posed at
the end of Act I, concerning the identity of the new ruler, the object
of Rodogune's secret love, and above all Cléopâtre's true intentions.

Act II belongs to Cléopâtre, being constructed around the
climactic Scene 3, in which she issues her ultimatum. But already
her opening monologue, with its incantatory grandiloquence, serves
to heighten the tension. This is the first of seven monologues which
form a notable feature of *Rodogune* (II, 1; III, 3, 6; IV, 2, 5, 7; V, 1).
Such is Cléopâtre's dissimulation that this form of 'direct communi-
cation' is needed, if the audience is to keep abreast of her changing
states of mind and intentions. In Scene 2, she torments the trusting
Laonice with a kind of rhetorical cat-and-mouse game which
contributes to the suspense:

Sais-tu que mon secret n'est pas ce que l'on pense? (439)

Cléopâtre's expert stage-management of this scene and the next
underlines the histrionic streak in her character. Her hatred of
Rodogune, she now reveals, is wholly political: her adversary's real
crime is to have threatened to steal the 'délices de *son* coeur' (476) —
not Demetrius Nicanor, of course, but the throne she has taken over
from him. This Cléopâtre intends to hold on to come what may.
Laonice says nothing of the princes' feelings for Rodogune, and the
fact that Cléopâtre remains ignorant of them will influence the
course of the plot during the whole central part of the play; it
produces a major detour in the action, during which the Queen will
pursue the illusory goal of recruiting one of her sons for her plot to
destroy Rodogune. Her ignorance thus forms a kind of retarding
device, such as is needed in a tragic plot propelled by such
destructive fury as hers. The Queen is full of self-confidence as she
confronts her sons in Act II, Scene 3. Her profound hypocrisy serves
to prolong the suspense, that is to delay as long as possible the
formulation of her appalling proposal: for maximum dramatic effect,
this has to be unveiled in stages. Cléopâtre at first presents the throne
she has so piously preserved for one of her sons as their joint
inheritance (525-26, 533, 539, 580). But every gloss she now puts on

the past evokes ironical echoes in the audience's mind, so flagrant
are the contradictions between what the Queen now alleges and what
we have been told already. (Compare for instance 544-50 with 455-
62, and 526 with 470-74.) Filial respect is the keynote of Antiochus's
reply: he begs his mother to say no more of their father's sad fate,
adding that neither he nor his brother is eager to inherit the throne
(590-600). Séleucus echoes this sentiment more briefly, and in view
of the princes' apparent diffidence, Cléopâtre decides to force the
pace, suggesting that they hesitate to accept the crown because they
loathe the prospect of the marriage that must go with it. In a
preposterous travesty of the truth, she blames the literally bewitching
charms of her enemy for the crime that ended Nicanor's life:

> Rodogune, mes fils, le tua par ma main. (630)

The scene is now set for the long-delayed, scandalous revelation
(642-45). A prolonged pause must follow, suggesting a gasp of
disbelief from the princes. Cléopâtre seems momentarily dis-
concerted by her sons' all too visible disarray. Soon, however, she
loses patience, and throws down the gauntlet brutally before
storming out:

> Ce n'est qu'en m'imitant que l'on me justifie. (668)

> Pour jouir de mon crime il le faut achever. (674)

The hour of decision is now upon the princes (Scene 4). Despite the
renewed 'mirror effect' of their parallel opening couplets (675-78),
their reactions are soon sharply differentiated. Séleucus's harsh but
lucid judgement arouses in him the will to revolt (745); but
Antiochus's filial piety produces only the desire to hide from the
truth by blaming Fate (688, 724). Séleucus's mysterious allusion to a
'beau dessein' that he has conceived (751) enables Corneille to end
Act II with his customary question mark — what is afoot?

The most obvious aspect of symmetry in *Rodogune* is the
elaborate parallel between Acts II and III. Act III is in many respects
a re-run of its predecessor, with Rodogune taking the part of

Cléopâtre; it is built around her encounter with the princes, which this time occupies the fourth scene. Laonice's defection in Scene 1, in accordance with the promise she gave earlier (345-47), will enable Rodogune to seize the initiative. She greets Laonice's revelations with bitterly ironic echoes of the confidant's reassurances in Act I. (Compare 759-66 with 312, 329-34 and 339-46.) Laonice declines to give further advice, saying that she has committed enough treason already (779); this marks her virtual withdrawal from the action. She urges Rodogune to turn instead to her ambassador Oronte, who tells her (Scene 2) that she has just one effective weapon left, namely the princes' love for her — about which he seems rather better informed than Cléopâtre. He urges her to exploit this advantage, but his worldly-wise advice is promptly rejected by Rodogune in her monologue (Scene 3) as a 'lâche artifice' (843). She will put the princes' ardour to the test, but without tempting them or compromising herself in any way (850-54). The keynote of this monologue, which is vital for understanding the principles of Rodogune's conduct, is the sense of honour she attaches to her rank. Her behaviour so far has been governed by the terms of the treaty, but now that Cléopâtre has torn the treaty up, she is released from that obligation:

> J'ose reprendre un coeur pour aimer et haïr (881)

Rodogune calls first upon the spirit of Nicanor, with such solemnity that she seems almost to conjure up his ghost before her (855-66). She begs his forgiveness for having neglected her duty of revenge, and vows to defend her own life, which is all that survives of his (876). She next addresses the unidentified 'cher Prince' who is the present object of her love, trembling at the thought of the ordeal she must impose upon him (883-92). Trepidation is indeed what she feels as the brothers approach.

Scene 4 begins in a low key, with a respectful plea by Antiochus that Rodogune choose the new king simply by naming the man she loves (413-14). She knows of Cléopâtre's evil designs, but the princes do not know that she knows, and she exploits this advantage with some skill. At first she declines to subvert the Queen's authority (940), saying that she intends to give her no pretext for renewed violence, and takes refuge behind 'l'ordre des traités' (934). More outspoken as usual than his brother, Séleucus declares that the throne is their joint inheritance, and that one of them has a perfect right to bestow his share in it on his brother (963-66). Rodogune replies with ominous words: they may have cause to regret her choice, if they force her to make one; but her unimpressed suitors, in neatly patterned dialogue (999-1010), insist on putting the onus on her. This she now accepts, and her final speech (1011-46) develops in a manner very similar to Cléopâtre's at the end of Act II, Scene 3 (615-60). Here the parallel between the two females is at its most evident; both Cléopâtre and Rodogune must appear equally cruel, equally uncompromising, equally full of hatred.

It is now that the solidarity between the two brothers begins to crumble. Scene 5 of Act III contains some of the most carefully patterned dialogue in the whole play, but this serves to express sharply contrasting reactions. The *romanesque* Antiochus, in the face of despair (1070-80), clings to his faith in human nature and in his own ability to move and persuade. In contrast, Séleucus the realist denounces not only the women's injustice, but that of Heaven itself (1051). His renewed attitude of revolt (1062; cf. 745) prompts him to attempt to withdraw from the fray (1110). The brief monologue with which Antiochus concludes Act III expresses his refusal to accept his brother's renunciation. His ominous words (1124-26) serve to end Act III on an appropriate note of foreboding.

Act IV marks the parting of the ways for the two brothers. Unlike the two preceding acts, it is built around not one, but two major encounters (Scenes 3 and 6) in which Antiochus and Séleucus in turn confront their mother. Scene 1, however, is almost as important, and it is focused above all on Antiochus. At first he continues to urge Rodogune to name the object of her love, and thereby the next King. In reply, she reiterates her recent grim command, claiming that her voice is the spirit of Nicanor demanding revenge (1172-74). He thereupon declares that if his mother's blood must flow, let it be from *his* veins. Now Rodogune, moved by his perfect chivalry, can no

longer hide her true feelings, and confesses that it is Antiochus
whom she loves, for he has done what she ideally expected of him:

> Votre refus est juste autant que ma demande:
> A force de respect votre amour s'est trahi,
> Je voudrais vous haïr s'il m'avait obéi...          (1220-22)

This effectively annuls her deadly order, and now she can see but
one solution, which is to return 'sous les lois que m'impose la paix'
(1225), and let Cléopâtre choose her successor by revealing the order
of the princes' birth; thus they will still have a fifty-fifty chance of
happiness. Antiochus is overjoyed, for his brother's sake as much as
for his own. Rodogune, however, cannot now contemplate the
prospect of losing him.

In the brief monologue forming Scene 2, Antiochus also
expresses ardent hope. This forms a transition to his next encounter,
which is with his mother (Scene 3). Almost at once, she announces
that his brother has forestalled him by obeying her command, and
that now there is but one remedy: fratricide (1276-72). He clearly
does not believe her, but in a clumsy and starry-eyed appeal to her
pity, he confesses that both he and his brother are in love with her
enemy. At once he has to bear the full brunt of her astonished fury
(1324-25). He once more appeals to her, offering his life to appease
her wrath (1339-48) — the same gesture as in his recent encounter
with Rodogune. This time, however, the mother seems to be moved
by his entreaties (1339-48), and Antiochus is naïve enough to take
her at her word, noticing neither her eagerness to be rid of him, nor
the ambiguity of her final words (1375-76). Quickly despatching
Laonice to fetch Séleucus (Scene 4), Cléopâtre now utters a brief but
indispensable monologue (Scene 5), in which she can speak only of
her rage and hatred, and of her scorn for Antiochus's gullibility.

When Séleucus arrives (Scene 6), Cléopâtre at once tries to
unnerve him, in the same manner as his brother earlier; but thanks to
his new-found serenity, he is able to stand his ground and reply with
calm self-confidence, denouncing his mother's hypocrisy and
declaring that he will never forsake his brother (1472-74). In a

further monologue (Scene 7), Cléopâtre is forced for the first time to admit defeat. In an interesting psychological development, she is shown as torn between amazement at Séleucus's disinterestedness (which clearly does not fall within her definition of human nature) and rage at the frustration of her plans. All the factors that have been retarding the catastrophe since Act II are thus removed: Cléopâtre realises that both her sons love Rodogune, and each other, more than they desire the throne, and that each one poses a very real threat to her power (1496). Everything is now in place for the final confrontation.

Act V is not only the climax of the play, it is the only act in which anything irreversible occurs — that is, if we include within it the preceding interval, for we learn from the Queen's opening soliloquy that Séleucus has just paid for his defiance with his life. The real function of this scene, however, is rhetorical: it forms yet another celebration of Cléopâtre's diabolical splendour. Her plans are revealed in an elaborate apostrophe to the poison she holds (1503-09): murder has now become a matter of self-defence, of survival even (1523-24), but above all of fidelity, to her own evil self and to the one true attachment of her life, the throne (1529-32). She has to don her mask again quickly as Laonice arrives (Scene 2) with a description of the now imminent marriage ceremony (1539-58). This serves both to enhance the effect of 'pompe' essential to Act V, and to underscore the isolation of Cléopâtre.

The happy couple now appear (Scene 3). After an exchange of compliments, there follows one of the most elaborate stage directions in the entire theatre of Corneille, setting the scene precisely and highlighting the changed order of precedence in the seating of the characters (1572-73). Soon the poisoned chalice is presented to Antiochus. He twice hesitates to drink on account of Séleucus's absence. This supreme moment of suspense heralds the major *coup de théâtre* of the play: in bursts Timagène with the news of the death of Séleucus. Here realism is obviously sacrificed to dramatic effect: the improbable wording of the dying man's reference to 'une main qui nous fut bien chère' (1643) is designed to cast equal suspicion on Cléopâtre and Rodogune, a fact which Antiochus, torn between grief

and horror, underscores heavily (1663-68). The stage is now set for
the final battle of the two Amazons, towards which the play's
symmetry has been leading us. Cléopâtre resorts almost entirely to
venomous accusation; Rodogune's arguments are more subtle and
varied. Before she can finish, however, the desperate Antiochus has
ceased to listen and is reaching once again for the chalice (1771-72).
His one aspiration is now to join his brother in death; but Rodogune
stays his hand. This is the cue for the final *coup de théâtre*, the
second major *péripétie* of this scene, which is Cléopâtre's literally
suicidal gamble with the poisoned wine. Her dying utterance is a
malediction of the survivors and a final explosion of satanic pride
(1821-24).

Now the tension subsides, as Cléopâtre is led away to die off-
stage, according to classical convention. The bewildered Antiochus
orders mourning drapes in place of the nuptial garlands, and all
further wedding plans to be postponed until the gods are appeased.
As to whether he and Rodogune 'lived happily ever after', this is left
to our conjecture.

*Rodogune* is one of Corneille's greatest achievements in the
realm of pure stagecraft, combining dramatic tension and shocks
with more subtle effects of paradox resulting from a skilful blend of
symmetry and contrast. The twin brothers stand together at the
centre of the play's symmetry, united by deep fraternal affection but
gradually forced apart by amorous rivalry, by difference of
temperament, but above all (from the dramatist's point of view) by
the imperious demands of the plot. They are caught in the cross-fire
between the 'mighty opposites', Cléopâtre and Rodogune, who
despite their enmity are led at times to adopt ironically similar
patterns of behaviour.

So far as unity of time is concerned, the author placed the plot
of *Rodogune* among those of his invention that for their realistic
enactment would require little more than the two hours of actual
performance time in the theatre (2, p.73). Unity of place gives rise to
a problem, for conspiratorial drama, in which one half of the cast is
plotting against the other half, is notoriously difficult to confine
realistically to one room of a palace. In *Rodogune* as in *Cinna*,

Corneille allowed the action to alternate between two distinct locations, but avoided drawing the audience's attention to this fact. A non-committal setting is therefore needed, what the author called 'une fiction de théâtre', consisting of a conventional meeting-place for the characters, who are presumed to enjoy the same confidentiality there as in their own bed-chamber (2, pp.78-79). Such problems caused much ink to flow in the seventeenth century, but today they are rightly passed over to the producer and designer. As for unity of action, it is hard to fault the plot of *Rodogune* as a close-knit dramatic structure. Cléopâtre's offensive in Act II provokes Rodogune's counter-attack in Act III, leading to Antiochus's vain attempts at reconciliation and to Cléopâtre's equally vain attempts to set one brother against the other in Act IV. The failure of her plan is the direct cause of her murder of Séleucus, the premature discovery of which frustrates the Queen's final attempt to eliminate her successors in Act V.

The plot is therefore the dominating element, and it has been constructed with minute care. *Rodogune* is indeed 'une pièce bien faite'. It could also be regarded as the classical counterpart of nineteenth-century melodrama, albeit of a rather superior, 'psychological' kind. The distinction between the innocent characters and the wicked one is sharper than almost anywhere else in Corneille. It presents several memorable confrontations between evil triumphant and the bemused representatives of virtue. In her monologues especially, Cléopâtre achieves a splendidly melodramatic role. Laonice plays the conventional part of 'turn-coat', of 'traitor' in the villain's camp, led by moral indignation to change sides. Finally, the villain loses patience, choosing to destroy herself, in a wild gamble, with the weapon she had prepared for her victims. The diction also tends towards the melodramatic, as in certain uses of the verb 'trembler' (424-26, 1018), and the sinister ambiguity of some of Cléopâtre's lines (e.g. 1375-76). But Corneille has taken great pains to make his characters' motivation more subtle and more convincing than in most melodrama. If we apply this term to *Rodogune* despite the anachronism, it must not be in any pejorative sense.

*iv) Not just a 'Spectacular'?*

However expert Corneille was at sending palpitations through the *parterre*, he did not limit himself to this perspective. Other ingredients of this tragedy were intended to appeal to the more discerning members of the audience. Indeed, this play contains a blend of ingredients which have sometimes been judged aesthetically incompatible. For example, however agile its stagecraft, *Rodogune* is also a highly rhetorical work, which like its predecessor *Pompée* could be seen as a stylistic 'regression' towards a pre-classical or even a Renaissance model (*41*). If it was the epic Lucan who presided over the grandiose narratives of *Pompée*, then it was surely the turgid Seneca whose presence is felt in certain passages of *Rodogune*:

> Serments fallacieux, salutaire contrainte,
> Que m'imposa la force et qu'accepta ma crainte,
> Heureux déguisements d'un immortel courroux,
> Vains fantômes d'Etat, évanouissez-vous!
> Si d'un péril pressant la terreur vous fit naître,
> Avec ce péril même il vous faut disparaître,
> Semblable à ces voeux dans l'orage formés,
> Qu'efface un prompt oubli quand les flots sont calmés.
> Et vous, qu'avec tant d'art cette feinte a voilée,
> Recours des impuissants, haine dissimulée,
> Digne vertu des rois, noble secret de cour,
> Eclatez, il est temps, et voici notre jour. (396-406)

The meaning of these lines is that the constraint and fear that had forced Cléopâtre to swear 'deceitful oaths' (by signing the treaty) have now vanished; the field is now clear for the return of her anger and hatred. She is preparing to tear up this treaty for, as she tells us a few lines further on, 'Le Parthe est éloigné, nous pouvons tout oser' (409). The literal sense of these lines may well prove elusive to an unprepared spectator; yet, in their high-flown semi-obscurity, how appropriate they are to Cléopâtre's celebration of herself as High

Priestess of Evil! Similar invocations occur in her last monologue (V, 1); and in her final tirade (1811-24), we find Corneille imitating the more frenzied type of 'Senecan' rhetoric. Rodogune prepares herself in a similarly portentous manner to present her own ultimatum to the Princes. In her monologue (especially lines 855-62), the elaborate rhetorical figures (dominated once more by invocation to personified feelings) are suggestive of the constraint which Rodogune has to exercise over her more spontaneous emotions. Like Cléopâtre, she is addressing her own anger and hatred and as she invokes the shade of the murdered king, crying out for revenge (863-82), the effect is almost one of incantation.

All these passages occur in a monologue, a device going out of fashion in 1645, and here used extensively for the last time by Corneille. (There is only one short one in *Nicomède*.) It serves to underline the isolation of the characters as well as the atmosphere of conspiracy and distrust; it also contributes to the high rhetorical 'pitch' of the play. The lofty nature of the thought or sentiment is enhanced by the giant strides of the successive quatrains of which several soliloquies, and notably Cléopâtre's first one, are largely made up.

The play's symmetries are also reinforced by the use of pattern rhetoric. Carefully balanced dialogue is used in particular to underline the complementary roles of Antiochus and Séleucus (e.g. 134-50, 349-56, 675-78, 999-1010, 1047-66). Rhetorical symmetry serves equally well to emphasise the growing divergence between their inclinations, as well as the harmony of their mutual affection. Their contrasting reactions to the Queen's ultimatum are expressed in successive utterances of two, eight and seventeen lines apiece (675-728). In the corresponding scene of Act III, the patterning is less rigid but still recognisable. Some of the play's themes are enhanced by the systematic use of echo lines. Often the effect is one of irony, as when Rodogune bitterly recalls Laonice's assurances about Cléopâtre's change of heart. In other cases, a motif is highlighted by means of a 'theme and variations' technique, as with references to the right of primogeniture ('Le droit d'aînesse': see 644, 699, 914, 968, 1291-92, 1423-24). Another motif, opposing *l'amour* and *la nature*, gains prominence towards the end of the play, and we note other forms of repetition, few of which can be accidental. (See lines 1130/1250-52/1257/1324/1362-64; cf. lines 148-49; 170/197-98; 163/747; 443/503/1011; 670/1045; 866/889; 986/1142; 1270/1274.)

The rhetoric deployed in *Rodogune*, and especially in the role of Cléopâtre, is a skilful blend of rational argument expounded in structured oratory, and of impassioned outbursts in which a 'beau désordre' represents the collapse of mental composure under the impact of violent emotion. Cléopâtre's 'ultimatum scene' offers the best example of this combination of techniques (*17*, ch.7). One effect of these rhetorical devices is to intensify the impression of 'pompe', that is of ritual grandeur. This concept is evoked in the very first line of the play ('Enfin ce jour pompeux...'); it is enshrined in the staging of Act V, and is finally recalled in Antiochus's command that the 'pompe nuptiale' be transformed 'en funèbre appareil' (1842). On the debit side, such effects are not always achieved without obscurity, particularly in Corneille's handling of personal pronouns and possessives.[3] However, an audience will generally put up with some such blemishes in a dramatic text that operates on a high level of eloquence.

Another ingredient of *Rodogune* consists of the kinds of situation, sentiment and language to which we apply the blanket term *romanesque*. The traditions, conventions and themes involved were all to be found in the popular novels of the time. Of these, Mlle de Scudéry's *Ibrahim ou l'illustre Bassa* (1641) and La Calprenède's *Cassandre* (1642) are the most likely by their date to have been fresh in Corneille's mind at the moment of the composition of *Rodogune*. These novels were founded on a flimsy basis of historical fact and geographical reality, but the plot of each one is extravagantly fictitious. They are novels in the heroic tradition, full of knights who

---

[3] See e.g. lines 494 (does *le* refer to 'le peuple' or to 'un roi'?); 522 (does *un seul* mean 'un seul mal' or 'un seul homme'?); 882-84 (the quick repetition of *toi* with reference to two different people is confusing); 1765 (does *mes attentats* mean 'ceux dont je pourrais être victime' or 'ceux que vous m'attribuez'? *Vos attentats* would make better sense; one or two editors have adopted this reading.)

recognise no man as their equal in valour, yet who live in meek submission to their lady's will — a will ruled by a rigid code of honour, requiring endless acts of 'submission' by the lover before his ardour can be acknowledged, let alone requited. Such influences are easily recognisable in *Rodogune*. The characters are faced with choices more complex and subtle than were those of Horace or Auguste (*37*). Antiochus and Séleucus have to resolve the conflicting claims of filial piety, fraternal affection and chivalrous love. Rodogune has to contend with a whole hierarchy of superimposed and conflicting duties which make paradoxical demands on her. She conceals her feelings for Antiochus until he has passed a kind of test of chivalry. Any thought of physical fulfilment of their love is subordinated to its spiritual exaltation — a distinctly *précieux* order of priorities. Complex considerations of duty, honour and prestige may produce decisions in conflict with obvious self-interest. In addition, there is the mystery of the order of the princes' birth.

Above all, the nature of love itself can be seen to have evolved in *Rodogune*. The idea of love's supremacy (e.g. 149-54) is important in this play, and it is associated with that of love's irrationality, as expressed in Rodogune's often-quoted quatrain on the 'elective affinities':

Il est des noeuds secrets, il est des sympathies
Dont par le doux rapport les âmes assorties
S'attachent l'une à l'autre et se laissent piquer
Par ces je ne sais quoi qu'on ne peut expliquer. (359-62)

Love is not only seen as irrational but as irresistible (829-32, 842). The concept of *amour-estime*, so prominent in *Le Cid*, seems to have been largely forgotten here, except in Rodogune's confession of love to Antiochus (1220-24); but that equally *romanesque* theme of love's obligations, of the acquisition of *mérite* through *services*, is much in evidence. The beloved tends to become almost the object of a religious cult: Rodogune's love for one of the princes is described as 'ce miracle', and her words are 'l'oracle' (1143-44); she is reverently called upon by her suitors to choose her husband and king, and she

responds in the chivalrous manner by imposing a veritable 'quest' on
those who aspire to her hand. In many parts of the play, what we
conventionally call 'Cornelian psychology' has undergone much
refinement, not to say rarefaction. The effect of Antiochus's
proposed self-sacrifice, for instance, will be the supreme paradox: 'Je
mourrai de douleur, mais je mourrai content' (1242). Voltaire was
predictably irritated: 'Avouons que ni dans *Cyrus*, ni dans *Clélie*, on
ne trouve point de sentences amoureuses d'une semblable afféterie'.[4]
Here Corneille was simply following recent fashion, and this fashion
did not outlast him.

### v) The Problem of 'Vraisemblance'

Historically speaking, the most controversial aspect of *Rodogune* has
been its alleged offences against *vraisemblance*. On this issue
Corneille distanced himself from the 'orthodox' critics, in particular
from d'Aubignac. The concept of *vraisemblance* was crucial, since it
involved a dramatist's whole conception of his art. Corneille
maintained, as we have seen, a distinction between on the one hand
the *sujet*, i.e. the central events of the plot, or the *effet*, i.e. the
catastrophe, which could be as extraordinary as one liked provided
one had the backing of history or classical myth; and on the other the
*acheminements* or *circonstances*, which must be plausible or at least
logical, that is either *vraisemblables* or *nécessaires*, following
Aristotle's distinction. But in *Rodogune* it was some of Corneille's
own inventions that appeared to lack verisimilitude. It is not likely
for instance that two grown-up twin princes would be left ignorant of
the order of their birth, since this determined their claim to the
throne. In fact d'Aubignac, whose literal-minded realism might have
been expected to find endless objections to the plot of *Rodogune*,
criticised only the entrusting of the exposition to a *confidente*, and
the speed with which the poison takes effect in Act V; but the bulk
of *La Pratique du théâtre* had already been written some time before
Corneille's play appeared (2, p.257, notes 5, 7, 13). A more vigorous

---

[4]*Commentaires sur Corneille* (25, vol. 54, p.490). Voltaire is referring here
to the two best-known novels of Mlle de Scudéry.

discussion of the actions of Rodogune herself is found in a letter of Saint-Evremond published in 1705. He defends the 'barbaric' command given by the princess to her suitors, not only as an act of legitimate self-defence, but also on grounds of historical and geographical authenticity, i.e. *la vérité des moeurs*.[5] *Vraisemblance* remained the central issue in the two principal assaults delivered on the play in the eighteenth century, those of Voltaire and Lessing. Voltaire was severe on *Rodogune*, but he admitted that the role of Cléopâtre, when well performed, could make a formidable impression (25, vol. 54, pp.529-31). His overall judgement seems to have been that some admirable passages and a superb last act had been achieved at the price of intolerable absurdities earlier in the play. His whole approach is dominated by a 'naturalism' quite foreign to the spirit of classical tragedy as we now see it, and not a little surprising, given his own extensive experience of the theatre. Lessing at least had an axe to grind: in his *Hamburgische Dramaturgie*, he singled out *Rodogune* as the supreme example of the sterile aesthetic traditions from which he sought to free the German stage. He assailed Corneille's play, admired in his own day (so he asserted) as 'the greatest masterwork of the greatest tragic poet' — an interesting judgement — on grounds of both morality and verisimilitude.[6] Later critics, in their pronouncements on *Rodogune*, tended to line up for or against the Voltaire-Lessing verdict. A more modern view is that this whole controversy about *vraisemblance* of plot or motive misses the real point of creative drama, or of narrative generally. These are now seen as essentially arbitrary constructions, in which the artist need not attempt to mirror 'real life'; what merits critical investigation is the function of each episode, of each detail if need be, in relation to the total structure, the end-product, the author's recognisable goal.

What then was Corneille's principal aim in constructing the plot of *Rodogune*? In the *Examen*, he appears particularly proud of

---

[5] Saint-Evremond, *Œuvres en prose*, edited by R. Ternois (Paris, Didier, STFM, 1969), IV, pp.423-25.
[6] Lessing, *Hamburgische Dramaturgie*, edited by O. Mann (Stuttgart, 1963), pp.117-29, 325.

the progressive effect of climax from one act to the next. Clearly the two main objectives Corneille set himself concern the final scene (which occupies well over half the fifth act). The first, as Voltaire correctly surmised, was to make the play's outcome as difficult as possible for the 'ideal' audience to guess, and for as long as possible. The second was to make the dilemma of Antiochus, when the reported words of the dying Séleucus improbably[7] fail to name his murderer, as convincing and consequently as tragic as possible. The symmetrical design of the whole plot was the essential thing here; but from a common-sense point of view, there seems to be every reason why Antiochus should suspect his mother rather than his beloved, and that his suspicions should be reinforced by Cléopâtre's erratic and inconsistent methods of self-defence — at least until she swallows the poison herself. However, Corneille suggests that Antiochus's agonised indecision is a product of his own exemplary *générosité*. This idealistic prince refuses on principle to think ill of his mother, because he values filial piety as highly as his love for another woman, and also because his perfect moral rectitude has made him sadly gullible. Although he knows that his mother has committed at least one other murder in the past, he has been completely taken in by her pretence of forgiveness and reconciliation in Act IV, Scene 3. This is a fine example of Corneille's handling of motivational problems. He endeavours to explain the less plausible actions in terms of traits of character already established. This is no doubt the most valid aspect of *vraisemblance* for us today, for although we may no longer look for fully rounded human beings in dramatic characters, we are still rightly concerned that they should present a coherent framework for a performer's interpretation. For the rest, the practical problem posed by *vraisemblance* — as Corneille well knew and as even Voltaire sometimes admitted — consisted of making sure, as far as possible, that the audience didn't notice the inconsistency or the improbability.

---

[7] Even in the case of this obviously contrived effect, verisimilitude is still a matter of subjective judgement, as J. Scherer has neatly demonstrated (*21*, p.372). On Corneille's handling of this scene, see also J. Vier (*44*, pp.5-6).

To what extent, then, is it true that in *Rodogune* Corneille has sacrificed character to plot and to the production of theatrical emotion? On this issue, critics are still quite sharply divided even today. Some take it for granted that 'psychology' has gone completely by the board in this play, for instance Descotes: 'Corneille se soucie beaucoup moins de vraisemblance psychologique que de faire rebondir une intrigue à laquelle il a donné tous ses soins' (*14*, p.250). Yarrow (*26*, p.114) on the other hand refers enthusiastically to the 'political and psychological realism' of *Rodogune*, whilst Adam (*9*, II, pp.360-61) stoutly defends the verisimilitude of the two female protagonists. Jasinski (*36*, p.212) sees in Scherer's claim (*3*, pp.xxi-xxii) that the character of Rodogune has been sacrificed to the needs of the plot, the intolerable implication that 'le grand Corneille' was professionally incompetent! Clearly the main characters in *Rodogune*, and especially the title-role, give rise to genuine difficulties of interpretation. A closer look at each one in turn may help us to pin-point and perhaps resolve them.

*vi) The Characters*

Cléopâtre presents few problems, for she is one of Corneille's most complete 'monomaniacs'. She gives few signs of inner conflict: the hesitation caused by her residual maternal instincts lasts exactly two-and-a-half lines (1509-11). Her 'character' is also relatively straightforward because it is presented rhetorically rather than naturalistically: her role consists of a series of resounding set-pieces rather than a serious exercise in dramatic psychology. In her death as in her life, Cléopâtre seeks to offer — to herself as well as to the attendant world — a spectacle of unparalleled magnificence in evil, and it is an aesthetic rather than an ethical judgement that we are invited to make on this demonic queen.

Her portrayal is a study of ferocious energy, of 'grandeur d'âme' unleashed in its most brutal form; it is devoid of any moral awareness, in so far as morality implies a limitation of the ego. For Cléopâtre does have an ethic of sorts, which is special to her conception of royalty, which represents in her eyes the supreme form of liberty, that is the negation of any idea of restraint. She sees power as absolute freedom, the limitless exercise of *bon plaisir*. When Séleucus points out the arbitrary nature of her favouritism, she explodes with indignation (1463-66). She jealously safeguards the secret of her sons' birth, aware of the god-like power it confers on her (444-51). Retention of this power in its every form is her over-riding motive. She burns with jealous hatred for Rodogune, not because Demetrius Nicanor had loved her, but because he crowned her as his queen. Had Cléopâtre not murdered him, he would have returned to depose her; this was his sole offence in her eyes (463-68). And now Rodogune threatens once again to supplant her by marrying whichever of her sons succeeds to the throne.

As a tragic heroine, Cléopâtre is the absolute negation of the Aristotelian concept of 'middling good character', of a person 'neither wholly good nor wholly bad', for she is given over entirely to evil. She stands foremost among the characters Corneille had in mind when proposing his unorthodox interpretation of the Aristotelian concept of *bonté* as 'le caractère brillant et élevé d'une habitude vertueuse ou criminelle', and she provides the principal illustration of it:

> Cléopâtre, dans *Rodogune*, est très méchante; il n'y a point de parricide qui lui fasse horreur, pourvu qu'il la puisse conserver sur un trône qu'elle préfère à toutes choses, tant son attachement à la domination est violent; mais tous ses crimes sont accompagnés d'une grandeur d'âme qui a quelque chose de si haut, qu'en même temps qu'on déteste ses actions, on admire la source dont elles partent. (2, p.14)

*Admirer* here simply means 'to be amazed', like the Latin *mirari*. Faced with such 'sublime' inhumanity, Corneille's audience is expected to experience a kind of horrified fascination; obviously no moral approval is implied.

Cléopâtre is indeed 'une héroïne en mal', not only wedded to violence, but also a liar and a hypocrite. Ties of blood have no meaning for her; whenever a close relative poses a threat to her power, she reaches for the dagger or the poison. She even incites Antiochus to fratricide (1267-70). Her lack of scruples is obvious; but how convincing are her tactics? Should we see her as a master schemer, 'froidement calculatrice', as Adam asserts (*9*, II, pp.361-62)? Voltaire, on the other hand, accused her of reckless imprudence, in presenting her ultimatum so brutally to her sons. If they could perform such a deed for the sake of a throne, who knows on whom they might practice it first? (Voltaire was right, of course, but a two-hour tragedy does not provide enough time for the precautions he had in mind.) However, there is clearly a flaw in Cléopâtre's Machiavellianism. Because her sex has been a constant handicap in her conquest of power, she harbours persistent feelings of insecurity, and her emotional vulnerability should be made apparent in a good interpretation (*33*, pp.232-33; *15*, pp.292-98). A rhetorical study of her part has shown how her frenzy is apt to upset the 'belle ordonnance' of her discourse (*17*, 179-91). Her calculations also misfire because she has no inkling of the nature of true *générosité*. She is genuinely, almost naïvely, astonished, at Séleucus's detachment from the objects of ambition (1433-50, 1475-82). She is blind because her lust for power has become an obsession, an 'almost carnal passion', as Couton puts it (*13*, p.114). Indeed, it is in such terms that she addresses the object of her lust, the throne (476). Such self-abandonment is intended to be seen as diabolical; Cléopâtre has pledged her soul to the forces of evil. In the face of Heaven, she breathes hatred and defiance (1523-32). Her self-inflicted fate is therefore quite in character: her gamble with the poison is an attempt to draw her 'enemies' after her into the abyss, and her final malediction culminates on a splendidly demonic note (1823-24).

Likewise the role of the twin princes has not provoked much controversy. There is a widely held view that the passivity of Antiochus and Séleucus, whatever its moral merits, lacks dramatic force, and it has even been seen as the beginning of a progressive reversal of the roles of the sexes in Cornelian tragedy (*15*, pp.290-93). This impression is reinforced by their curious anonymity: the audience does not learn their names until Cléopâtre addresses each one in Act IV (1259, 1404). The princes' status as twins is of considerable importance in the plot. The uncertain order of their birth provides an element of mystery and suspense. They thus appear equally justified in their quest for the throne. Aware of their mytho-logical antecedents, they seek to model their relationship on the perfect attachment of Castor and Pollux, rather than on the eternal enmity of Eteocles and Polynices, or of Atreus and Thyestes (169-200). Such is their anxiety on this score that they take a solemn vow of fidelity (205-10). Throughout Act I, they tend to play the part of 'identical twins', preferring the 'nous' to the 'je' form. Subsequently, under the pressure of circumstances, they reveal contrasts of temperament and assume differing roles, but their mutual solidarity remains unaffected. Antiochus's exclamation, on learning of his brother's death, is poignant indeed:

O frère, plus aimé que la clarté du jour...(1653)

The symmetry of their personalities and roles forms an important part of the play's structure.

It is in their reaction to the cruel demands made of them that the contrasting natures of Antiochus and Séleucus emerge. Antiochus first refuses to examine his mother's part in his father's death (589-98), then to condemn her cruelty or even to look the truth in the face (II, 4). After hearing both ultimatums, he declines to condemn either woman, counselling infinite patience and hope (III, 5). He continues to treat Rodogune with chivalrous reverence, and finally wins her avowal of love with his offer of total self-sacrifice (IV, 1). In his interview with his mother (IV, 3), he speaks with rather more force (1290 ff.) but allows himself to be duped by Cléopâtre. Even when faced with the ultimate evidence of her evil, he still pleads with her to save herself from it (1810, 1825). In contrast, Séleucus loses no time in denouncing his mother's violence and his brother's forbearance, and thus displays a fair degree of realism. He is bold and direct in his address to Rodogune (955 ff.). His immediate reaction to her ultimatum, once he is free to speak his mind, is to withdraw from the fray with an attitude of 'a plague on both your houses' (III, 5). His last words to Cléopâtre, though never overtly disrespectful, are frank and harsh enough to seal his own fate (1467 ff.).

These contrasting reactions have been diversely judged. A modern 'realist' will no doubt be inclined to praise Séleucus for his lucidity and to see his conduct as 'truly generous' and 'more consistent and logical' (*33*, pp.232-33). Accordingly, it is Antiochus who must be judged the more naïve of the two. On the other hand, in a seventeenth-century perspective, Antiochus represents not only the 'parfait amant' according to the *romanesque* code, but also the exemplary Christian hero in his filial piety, his refusal to judge, his determination to preserve hope, and his willingness to forgive. By his self-sacrifice, he convinces Rodogune that he is worthy of her love. Thus Séleucus may be seen as the 'weaker' twin, bringing about his own death through despair, whereas Antiochus is finally rewarded for his pious steadfastness. Yet nowhere does he combine nobility of soul with shrewd judgement so admirably as does Séleucus in the closing lines of his role (1451-75). Ultimately, one might therefore be inclined to see the two princes as 'equal on points'.

The real difficulties, for producer, performer and critic alike, are those involved in the title role. The basic problem is evident: how to establish the unity of a character that Corneille depicts as virtuous and sensitive, and who nevertheless demands of her suitors an act of matricide as the 'price' of her hand. Many critics, following Voltaire's example, have judged her character to have been 'engineered' solely to meet the demands of the plot. Others have gone to great lengths to defend Corneille against a charge they consider damaging to his reputation.[8] A close reading of Rodogune's part is therefore required. How are its subtleties to be conveyed to a

---

[8] See above, p.35. The most searching studies of the personage of Rodogune are those of Jasinski (*36*); Georges (*31*); Goulet (*16*), pp.152-67, Herland (*35*) and Gossip (*33*), pp.235-39.

theatre audience? How can Rodogune appear both as an avenging
fury on the Electra model, and yet as a well-bred princess full of
*romanesque* sentiments and ideas? The only critic who has
envisaged this problem from a specifically theatrical angle despairs
of putting such complexities across on the stage: 'En réalité, ce qui
transparaît le mieux du caractère de Rodogune, c'est bien la haine
qu'elle éprouve pour Cléopâtre, [...] et les intentions secrètes que
Corneille prête au personnage dans l'*Examen* ne sont pas sensibles au
spectateur' (*14*, p.254). He is no doubt right, and yet the author
clearly tried very hard to make us aware of the complexities of her
role. His efforts suggest that he did not regard this play solely as a
'machine' for the production of theatrical emotion.

It is important initially to grasp the diplomatic and juridical
realities that govern Rodogune's conduct (see *1*, II, pp.1286-88).
Rigid constraints are placed on her by her status and situation. As
sister to King Phraates of the Parthians, the princess has become a
key figure, a 'gage de la paix' (872, 879) in negotiations between her
homeland and the neighbouring kingdom of Syria. That is why,
having once been betrothed to Demetrius Nicanor, she is now
destined to marry his successor; this is the obligation she refers to as
'l'ordre des traités' (934). But Cléopâtre has torn up the treaty; this is
the sole reason why Rodogune, at the insistent demand of the
princes, appears prepared to violate her treaty obligations by choosing one of them herself. But as her legalistic mind (a quality she
shares with Nicomède) sees it, she thereby at once reactivates a
previous duty, that of avenging the death of Nicanor. It is in exactly
these terms that she presents her situation, in the imagined presence
of his 'ombre', in her central monologue (866-82).

There is a basic difference between Cléopâtre's notion of
royalty and Rodogune's: the former sees the essence of power as
limitless, irresponsible freedom, whereas for the latter the first
implication of rank and authority consists of the obligations they
impose and the honour they confer. She declares that despite her
love for one of the princes, if destiny commands it, she will marry
the other: '...le devoir fera ce qu'aurait fait l'amour' (375). Here is an
outstanding example of Cornelian 'amour volontaire'. Pride she has

in plenty, which is why she spurns Oronte's advice that she exploit her 'sex-appeal' in her interview with the princes. She seems determined to keep them subservient to her and to retain the initiative — a strategy clearly formulated in her monologue (990-94), where she freely confesses to her *orgueil*. This is not just vanity, but an obligation placed upon her by her rank.

The same 'heroic pride' appears in another important scene, in which Antiochus 'passes the test', and the princess, moved by his exemplary self-sacrifice, admits that it is he whom she secretly loves. Although she does not even now withdraw her ultimatum, she confesses that she did not expect it to be obeyed (1220-29). Rodogune was in effect bluffing, hoping both to parry Cléopâtre's thrust and to maintain her own hold on her suitors, rather than simply destroy her enemy. This reading is confirmed by Corneille's statement in his *Examen*: 'Elle ne la fait pas [*la cruelle proposition*]...avec espoir de la voir exécuter par les princes, mais seulement pour s'exempter d'en choisir aucun, et les attacher tous deux à sa protection par une espérance égale' (5, p.144).

A logical account of Rodogune's motives can therefore be assembled from the evidence of the text; but there is a minor difficulty in the tender feelings she expresses not only for Antiochus, but also apparently for his late father. She invokes his spirit affectionately (III, 3), referring to him as 'chère ombre' (863) and to herself as 'les restes de ta vie' (876); and while still addressing Nicanor, she accuses Cléopâtre of seeking to 'percer ce sein infortuné [her own]/ Pour y chercher le coeur que tu m'avais donné' (877-78; cf. 1153-54). However, these passages taken together seem to indicate little more than a 'dutiful affection' for the memory of a man whose death has imposed on her a long-standing duty of revenge. What is her age, then? The text gives no clear indication, but no doubt the audience will prefer to suppose that there was a large gap in years between Rodogune and Nicanor, rather than between herself and her present suitors. Fortunately for the stage success of the play, these minor obscurities are apparent only on reflection.

An investigation of the principal roles in *Rodogune* suggests a three-part creative process. First of all, Corneille set out to invent a plot that would fascinate and amaze the audience. Next we can imagine him filling in the material details in order to create characters who could plausibly perform the actions demanded of them by the plot. Finally we see him making some small amendments to the text, and above all issuing *a posteriori* explanations (both in the *Examen* and in the *Discours*) in order to justify his work in the face of criticism. For his contemporaries, Corneille was the supreme inventor of plots, whereas Racine achieved fame as a creator of characters. Such was the view of Saint-Evremond (*Œuvres en prose*, ed. cit., IV, pp.429, 431). This opposition is not seen in such absolute terms today, and it is now customary to regard Corneille also as a master creator of character. However, we can see in a play like *Rodogune* the reasons for the seventeenth-century view.

### vii) Thematic Structure and Tragic Content

The plot looms so large in *Rodogune* that the play has often been found short of ideas. The rather unusual dilemmas faced by the characters seem to lack general relevance, and Couton for instance declares that in this play 'la pensée politique est inexistante' (*1*, I, pp.1282-83). Another view however is that Corneille intended it as an anti-Machiavellian drama, demonstrating the false calculations of tyrants like Cléopâtre who understand nothing about *générosité* (*23*, II, p.372). As a treatment of this particular theme, *Rodogune* is surely inferior to *Nicomède*. Yet it does have a thematic structure, or at least a pattern of recurrent motifs. The unusual power struggle which forms the plot is reflected in Corneille's choice of vocabulary. The verb *régner* occurs no less than thirty-seven times, which is impressive if not exceptional. More remarkable is the recurrent metaphoric use of the various symbols of royalty — the throne, the crown, the sceptre and the diadem. A rapid count (by O. de Mourgues, *41*) reveals that *trône* occurs no less than thirty-seven times, *couronne* fourteen (and the verb *couronner* eight times), whilst *sceptre* makes nine appearances and *diadème* eight.

A dominating presence in *Rodogune* is therefore that of the throne — a metaphor above all until the final act, when its physical presence on the stage is important. (See lines 87-96, 122-28, 135-40, 162-66, 304-09, 541-49, 742-46, 1084-88, 1529-30.) The symbolism of the crown is splendidly evoked in the opening lines of Cléopâtre's address to her sons (521-26), even though the object is not actually named. (See also lines 32, 211, 615-21, 683-84, 911-12, 963-66, 1259.) The sceptre and the diadem are explicitly linked together in the concluding lines of the Queen's first monologue (419-26; see also lines 76, 104, 177, 243-44, 449-50, 599-606, 796, 995, 1248, 1268, 1506-07). The characters' attitudes towards these symbols of royalty differ sharply. The passage just referred to is a splendid expression of Cléopâtre's compulsive lust for power, which elsewhere she formulates more briefly (e.g. 1268, 1529). As for Rodogune, she at first views the throne with apprehension, like the marriage that will set her on it (304-09). Later she insists on the obligations of duty and honour that govern her conduct as a princess, in pursuit of the trappings of royal authority (867-70; cf. 934-35, 1231-32). For their part, the princes view these emblems with greater detachment. They insist at first on the 'exchange value' of the throne, which each proposes to the other in return for the person of Rodogune (I, 3; III, 4, 963 ff.). Subsequently both Cléopâtre and Rodogune insist brutally on the 'price' that Antiochus or his brother must pay for the throne or the marriage that goes with it (642, 670, 742, 998, 1085). Inevitably the princes judge this 'price' excessive (681-86, 1084-90).

The insignia of royalty therefore play a significant, divisive role in *Rodogune*. Opposed to them is the triple source of human solidarity: *l'amitié*, *l'amour* and *la nature*. (This last term refers to the 'natural' emotions associated with ties of blood.) Antiochus and Séleucus are concerned to reconcile the first two: *l'amitié* and *l'amour* threaten to pull them apart, but their fraternal affection holds fast despite all the temptations. In Act I, Laonice describes the new situation created by the treaty: A présent que l'amour succède à la colère...' (343), a line which is ironically echoed by Rodogune (759); much of the rest of the play consists of putting this statement to the test. Not only is there a contest between *l'amour* and *l'amitié*, but for the brothers there is a clash between these values and the other one they prize, *la nature*, to which Antiochus at least remains wholly dedicated. Cléopâtre claims that 'Nature' confers on her an unconditional right to her sons' loyalty, and that their love for Rodogune is a betrayal of this. Hence her supreme piece of sophistry, branding them as *des fils dénaturés* (1325). Her only use for 'la nature' seems to be as an aid to deception (1362). These antithetical motifs form an important part of the play's symmetries and oppositions. (See also lines 81, 108 ff., 147 ff., 170, 181, 207, 687, 753-54, 916, 1117, 1130, 1239, 1250-58, 1476.)

As for tragic content, *Rodogune* visibly possesses all the formal qualities that (as we saw earlier) Corneille and his contemporaries associated with the term *tragédie*: five acts, characters of elevated rank, the unities and a serious action involving a major peril. A recent study, searching and erudite (*30*) has shown how the author contrived to transform a subject originally close to classical myth into a Christian tragedy. The plot, or parts of it — a mother seeking to kill her children, who are called upon to avenge the death of one parent on the other — has points of contact with the Medea legend as well as with the Orestes-Electra-Clytemnestra myth. Yet the end-product looks very different: an affirmation of human free-will and of the supremacy of Divine Providence. Cléopâtre's attempt to usurp quasi-divine power is frustrated by a Providential intervention in which human 'prudence' has its full part to play. It might be asked how explicit were Corneille's intentions in this respect. In his *Trois Discours*, he underlines the importance of 'poetic justice' — the rewarding of virtue and the punishment of vice — in achieving the moral function of tragedy. He refers in this context to the dénouement of *Rodogune*, stressing the importance of an alteration he made to history: Antiochus no longer forces his mother to drink the poison. Corneille sees this as vital to the moral lesson of the play: 'La punition de cette mère impitoyable laisse un plus fort exemple, puisqu'elle devient un effet de la justice divine, et non pas de la vengeance des hommes' (*2*, p.48). The same message is delivered in the play by Oronte (1831-36). Not only Corneille, but most of his contemporaries believed in treating their characters quite explicitly according to their moral deserts; even Racine hesitated to overturn this convention entirely.

However, Corneille was no simpleton, and the ending of *Rodogune* is neither facile nor over-optimistic. Its ambiguity is surely evident. The upright and innocent Séleucus suffers a cruel death, and the pious Antiochus, far from rejoicing in his own survival, is bitter to the point of casting doubt on heavenly justice (1771-80). As for Cléopâtre, her end can scarcely be called tragic, for she achieves a flamboyantly exultant death, a kind of diabolical apotheosis in which she remains triumphant (at least in her own eyes), cursing her would-be saviours and grinningly predicting the perpetuation of her evil race (1823-24). There is no recognition of guilt on her part, nor any reconciliation with the moral order that finally prevails. In this respect, the 'melodramatic' plot is sustained right to the end.

Thus the dénouement mirrors the play's presentation of good and evil. The contrasts are for the most part stark and simple: innocence versus guile, love versus hatred, moral idealism versus political opportunism. As a result, this tragedy may seem suited for the kind of allegorical interpretation that is fashionable in Corneille criticism today. If we see Cléopâtre as a symbolic figure, then the significance of her unrepentant end becomes clear: she is not just an extreme example of human perversity, but a literally Satanic figure, confident in her own evil immortality. Her sons and Rodogune strive not only to oppose and defeat her, but if possible to rescue her from her own demons. Together these three characters could be said to represent three possible Christian responses to the infernal challenge presented by Cléopâtre. The idealistic Antiochus opposes evil by turning the other cheek, by means of prayer and tearful entreaty, by refusing to judge, or to lose faith in the healing power of love, or in the wisdom of Providence. The uncompromising Séleucus has no such confidence; yet he too is intrepid in the face of evil, to which he responds with forthright denunciation and then by withdrawing from the fray — a reaction that might have led him, had he survived, to a life of contemplation rather than of action. But it is the 'prudent' Rodogune who proves to be the most effective ally of Providence:

while never renouncing or betraying love, she resolves to defeat evil force if possible with her own force, and to turn all her resources of worldly prudence to the defence of her life, her love, her rights and her values. On the surface, her actions may deceive — as is required by the symmetry of the plot — but her heart is not corrupted. Each of these separate paths represents a possible choice in the face of evil. But did Corneille present this striking spectrum of attitudes in order to lend didactic force to his play, or quite simply for increased dramatic effect? This is the kind of issue that divides critics today, and ensures that *Rodogune* will continue to provoke lively debate.

## 2. Nicomède

*i) Nicomède in the Theatre*

The first performance of *Nicomède* can be dated more precisely than
that of *Rodogune*, since a contemporary author of memoirs,
Mademoiselle de Montpensier, states that it was 'mise au jour
aussitôt après la liberté de Monsieur le Prince'. The Prince de Condé
was released from prison on February 13, 1651, and so it seems
likely that Corneille's play received its première before the end of the
same month. 'La représentation n'en a point déplu' wrote the author
in his preface *Au lecteur*; this seems confirmed by the delay in
publication, for although the *privilège* is dated 12 March 1651, the
first printing was not completed until November 21 of the same year.
This interval would have provided ample time for a successful first
run. As for the performers, it seems likely that Corneille remained
faithful to Floridor, who had recently transferred from the Marais to
the Hôtel de Bourgogne, and that *Nicomède* was therefore first
presented at the Hôtel. Floridor no doubt took the title role. Another
leading actor there, Montfleury, was ridiculed by Molière in
*L'Impromptu de Versailles* (1663) for his bombastic rendering of the
part of Prusias, which in all probability he had created twelve years
earlier (*1*, II, pp.1458-59).

*Nicomède* was to be Corneille's last enduring stage triumph. It
also achieved an immediate *succès de librairie*, further separate
editions being published in 1652 and 1653 (*6*, p.31). We know that
Molière chose the play for his company's first appearance before
Louis XIV and his court, on October 24 1658 — perhaps the most
crucial single performance of his career. He admired *Nicomède*, and
there are, as we shall see, several echoes of it in his works. The first

English translation of *Nicomède* appeared in 1671; we are told on the
title-page that it had been given the previous year at the Theatre
Royal, Dublin.[9] As for the Comédie Française, its records show that
this tragedy was performed ninety-four times there between its
foundation in 1680 and the end of the seventeenth century — several
times each year, in fact — and that it remained popular there until
1727, after which it was only intermittently revived. An almost total
eclipse during the mid-eighteenth century and the revolutionary
years was followed by quite a vigorous revival under the First
Empire and the Restoration. At this time *Nicomède* won favour with
its unusual variety of tone: Victor Hugo and Stendhal saw it as a
forerunner of *le drame romantique*. By the end of 1973, it had
received a total of 392 performances at the Comédie Française,
which puts it in seventh place — immediately after *Rodogune*, in
fact — in order of popularity among Corneille's works over three
centuries. (See above, p.9, note 1.) Among the most noted
interpreters of the title role were Baron, Grandval, Lekain, Talma,
Beauvallet and Albert Lambert (*14*, pp.260-66).

## ii) An Artful Invention

The evidence concerning the genesis of *Nicomède* suggests an
interesting problem: did it begin with an historical narrative out-
lining a plot, or with a more abstract vision of character traits, moral
attitudes and/or dramatic themes, that the author then sought to
embody in an historical situation? To judge from the lines translated
from Justin's *Historiae Philippicae* that Corneille included in his
preface *Au lecteur* (a text which nineteen years later, with a few
modifications, became the *Examen*: *8*, pp.38-40, 150-51), *Nicomède*
looks like a straightforward case of a drama based on an historical
narrative. Yet in the opening paragraph of this preface, the author
defines the essence of his drama in notably abstract terms:

---

[9] *Nicomède. A Tragi-Comedy translated from the French of Monsieur
Corneille*, by John Dancer. London, Roger L'estrange, 1671.

> La tendresse et les passions, qui doivent être l'âme des
> tragédies, n'ont aucune part en celle-ci: la grandeur de
> courage y règne seule et regarde son malheur d'un oeil si
> dédaigneux qu'il n'en saurait arracher une plainte. Elle y
> est combattue par la politique et n'oppose à ses artifices
> qu'une prudence généreuse... (*8*, p.38)

Then he adds: 'L'histoire qui m'a prêté de quoi la faire paraître en ce
haut degré est tirée de Justin' — a statement which suggests that
Corneille had searched among the ancient historians with a pre-
conceived object in view, and that in this passage of Justin he had
found exactly what he wanted.

Another possibility however is that Corneille's interest in this
subject had been triggered off by a work by a rival dramatist, namely
Rotrou's tragedy *Cosroès*, first performed probably in 1648. It
depicts the overthrow and death of Chosroes II, King of Persia, in
AD 628. He is ousted by his son, the heir apparent Syroès, who has
been forced into plotting this *coup* by the intrigues of his step-
mother, Syra, whose character and role clearly owe something to
Cléopâtre in *Rodogune*. The chief resemblance betwen *Cosroès* and
*Nicomède* however lies in the relationships basic to the plot: a weak
monarch is manipulated by his unscrupulous second wife, who seeks
to cast aside the legitimate heir, born of her husband's first marriage,
in favour of their own son. Yet there could hardly be a sharper
contrast between the two plays, as regards the personality and
actions of the hero, and the dénouement. Syroès is a vacillating and
conscience-striken plotter, who owes his survival to a kindly
Providence rather than to his own qualities or deeds, which are
utterly unheroic.[10]

It seems therefore that the author, having found the basis of his
plot in Rotrou, then discovered in Justin a new historical framework
in which he could insert this pattern of relationships. He next

---

[10] See *40*, and also my edition of *Cosroès* (*Textes littéraires*, University of
Exeter, 1983), pp.xxiv-xxv. Some twenty years later, Racine was to use the
situations and characters of *Nicomède*, in a strikingly similar operation, as
his point of departure in composing an equally different tragedy, *Mithridate*.

proceeded to make a number of alterations and additions to this historian's version of events, which he discusses in his Preface. He begins with the most obvious one, namely that in Justin Prusias's plot to kill his son is forestalled, and he is assassinated, by Nicomedes himself. 'J'ai ôté de ma scène l'horreur d'une catastrophe si barbare, et n'ai donné ni au père ni au fils aucun dessein de parricide' (8, p.38). This is not quite true of Prusias (see 1587-88); but Corneille transformed the son, who in history had been just as servile an ally of the Romans as his father, into an ardent nationalist and a perfect *généreux*. The author also endowed him with an undying hatred and defiance of Rome; he sees it almost as his mission to champion resistance to Rome throughout Asia Minor. In history, this had been the role not of Nicomedes II of Bithynia, but of Mithridates the Great, King of Pontus from 120 to 63 BC — the hero of Racine's tragedy — whose mantle Corneille places firmly on the shoulders of his own protagonist. Here, too, contemporary drama may have offered inspiration as well as the history books: in 1636, La Calprenède's tragedy *La Mort de Mithridate* had depicted not only the 'local resistance' to Roman expansionism, but the ruses of Roman diplomacy. Corneille also decided to give prominence to this theme.

This political dimension is embodied in a major character whom Corneille invented on the basis of a false historical analogy, namely the Roman envoy Flaminius. A certain Titus Quinctius Flamininus had indeed been sent to Bithynia, to demand the surrender of the fugitive Hannibal, who committed suicide rather than suffer this fate. However this had happened thirty-four years earlier, in the reign of Prusias I, father to our monarch. On this basis Corneille set up two more brilliant inventions: he supposes that the young prince Nicomède had been the pupil and disciple of Hannibal, and that the envoy was none other than the son of the general Caius Flaminius, whom Hannibal had trounced at the battle of Lake Trasimene in 217 BC, but who had no family ties with our ambassador. The personal enmity between Nicomède and Flaminius is thus greatly intensified. (It is not quite certain whether this 'confusion' was an historical sleight of hand or a genuine error on Corneille's part.)

As for Prusias himself, Corneille skilfully develops the portrait he found in Appian of a sycophant of the Romans, adding for good measure his subservience to the will of Arsinoé. The remaining characters are but shadows or mere names in Justin, and so Corneille was free to invent their character and role almost at will. Various other minor sources have been suggested,[11] but a dramatist of Corneille's talent scarcely needed obscure historical precedents to help him imagine a character like the 'noble turncoat' Attale. As for Arsinoé, her stage predecessors included both Cléopâtre and Rotrou's Syra; yet there is a distinct originality in her character, in the way that manipulative guile always prevails over the temptation to violence. Laodice is a fiction with an historical name, that of the princess whom Nicomedes II, according to Justin, married after becoming king. Whether historically accurate or not, each alteration or addition made by Corneille to Justin's account was put to a well thought-out purpose. All the details he selects or invents, all the liberties he takes with history, can be shown to be dramatically productive: they help animate situations or develop character along lines that are theatrically effective or symbolically significant. No dramatist ever shaped the raw material of history with a keener sense of purpose than did Corneille.

But was stage effect his sole concern? Or was *Nicomède* intended also as a comment on contemporary events and personalities? Mademoiselle de Montpensier not only gives us the date of the play's creation; she also sees a reference to Condé's arrest and imprisonment in the line: 'Quiconque entre au palais porte sa tête au roi' (94). This isolated line was expanded to 'quelques vers' by an eighteenth-century editor; but it was not until 1951 that a fully developed 'allegorical' interpretation of the play was proposed by Georges Couton in his controversial book *Corneille et la Fronde* (12). He argued that the persecuted hero was a portrait of the Prince

---

[11] In particular by L.M. Riddle, *The Sources and Genesis of Pierre Corneille's Tragedies from 'Médée' to 'Pertharite'* (Baltimore: Johns Hopkins Press, 1926).

de Condé, whose brilliant military career, as well as his status as Prince of the Blood, had made him seem menacing in the extreme when he set himself up in opposition to the Queen Regent, Anne of Austria, and her unpopular minister, Cardinal Mazarin. As a result he was imprisoned, together with two of his close kinsmen, in January 1650. But mounting political pressure, culminating in riots in Paris in early February 1651 (including a virtual siege of the Palais-Royal by the mob) forced Mazarin to release the prisoners a few days later. However, in view of Corneille's staunch royalism (for which there is plenty of evidence, including some lines of *Nicomède*) it is hard to admit that he would have declared support in this way for a rebellious nobleman. It has also been suggested that his self-confessed late alterations to his text (see *8*, p.51) had something to do with these preoccupations. Certainly the dramatist would have had to work fast in order to incorporate such allusions in time for the 'revised' *Nicomède* to be performed in that same month of February 1651, i.e. before the closure for Lent. So although this interpretation of the play is not absurd, nothing like proof has been offered for it, and it should be regarded with caution.

### iii) A Stirring Drama

*Nicomède* is less obviously 'theatrical' than *Rodogune*. There are no mysteries of birth or identity to intrigue the audience, no poisoned chalice to rivet its attention. The hero even seems somewhat under-employed. When the play begins, he has left his army and has come to court, he claims, in order to defend himself and Laodice; in fact he has walked into Arsinoé's trap. Successive blows rain down upon him, and he is gradually reduced to complete inaction. Yet we do not perceive him as crushed underfoot, so vigorous is his verbal self-defence and so buoyant his self-confidence. It is he who comes off best in the successive verbal duels which are just as essential to the action of the play as the events which constitute the plot, that is the confrontation of personalities and motives, and the clash between opposing policies, interests, moralities and beliefs (cf. *6*, p.10).

*Nicomède* begins with an advantage over *Rodogune* in that its exposition is impressively compact, lively and well-motivated. The first scene also presents two of the principal characters. Not only is all the necessary information supplied in one scene of average length, but an acute sense of danger is conveyed. Laodice stresses the sinister influence of Arsinoé, and mentions the unexpected return of Attale to the court of Bithynia. Nicomède's slightly impatient reply introduces one of the author's 'historical inventions', namely that Attale's return was part of a bargain Flaminius had struck with Arsinoé; in exchange, she had agreed to hand over the fugitive Hannibal, whom Nicomède refers to as 'mon maître' (30). The rhetorical pattern of this scene is a kind of extended antithesis, each character expressing confidence in his or her own safety, but alarm for the other. Nicomède fears for Laodice because of Arsinoé's unscrupulousness, a view which she neatly turns around in warning him not to rely on his father's 'natural' protective love (75). Nicomède, she perceives, has put himself in the wrong by his unauthorised return from the army to court, and has endangered himself as well:

> Vous n'avez en ces lieux que deux bras comme un autre.
>
> (92)

— a line denounced by Voltaire as a 'vers de basse comédie', but it might be seen as a sample of Laodice's down-to-earth realism. As the debate reaches its climax, Attale is seen approaching, and Nicomède's sudden plea:

> Il ne m'a jamais vu, ne me découvrez pas. (118)

comes as the first clear hint that *Nicomède* is not going to be the most solemn of tragedies.

By remaining incognito throughout Scene 2, Nicomède is in a position both to observe Attale's behaviour towards Laodice, and to make satirical jibes whenever he chooses. This scene, one of apparently good-humoured banter with an undercurrent of ferocity,

sets the tone for much of the play. Attale's allusion to the Roman
backing he enjoys gives Nicomède the cue for his first broadside of
sustained irony (156-82): how can Attale be counting for support, in
wooing a queen, on proud Roman republicans who despise crowned
heads? Attale understandably bids Laodice silence this insolent
servant of hers, but her only response is to resume the taunting
herself (205-12). The hero's incognito is being exploited to an extent
found rarely outside comedy (230-38); in fact the whole situation is
near the limit of plausibility. It is almost a relief when Nicomède
appeals to Arsinoé to identify him as soon she appears on stage
(Scene 3). His words are again charged with a rather sneering irony
(especially 244).

Arsinoé, however, does not immediately oblige. She replies
with an enquiry about the fate of the Prince's abandoned army (250).
Irony is closely linked to 'double entendre' in the ensuing bout of
shadow-boxing (256-62). Arsinoé's self-confidence suggests strongly
that she has a trump card up her sleeve. When Attale finally tumbles
to the stranger's identity (263), his apology is cut short by Nicomède,
who demands 'fair play' (one of his most insistent themes) in their
contest for the hand of Laodice. After his brusque departure, Arsinoé
upbraids her son (Scene 4) for his deference to Nicomède (278), then
sends him to summon Flaminius. The Queen is now left alone with
Cléone (Scene 5), and cynically reveals her machinations. This is her
'Connais-moi tout entière' scene (like *Rodogune*, II, 2); it is all the
more vital because Arsinoé, unlike Cléopâtre, is granted no
'confession' monologue. She now explains that she has not taken
Attale into her confidence because she fears the effects of his
'virtuous' Roman education (288-92). The brazen cynicism of her
ensuing declaration (295 ff.) puts Arsinoé momentarily on a par with
Cléopâtre. Voltaire found this confession revolting, but Corneille's
art was not so squeamish. Cléone doubts that the Romans are so
idealistic as Arsinoé imagines; but the Queen replies that she and
Flaminius alone were responsible for the death of Hannibal.
Corneille thus 'whitewashes' the Romans collectively for a crime
often laid at their door. Continuing the revelation of her ruses,
Arsinoé admits to having used Flaminius to stir up Roman hostility

to the long-arranged marriage between Nicomède and Laodice (314-23), and that she has lured Nicomède away from the army so that he may be left isolated and defenceless. She partly reveals the role of Métrobate in her machinations, but this information is deliberately left incomplete for the time being. The end of Act I therefore provides the audience with plenty of curiosity and suspense, so formidable is the 'machine' that Arsinoé has mounted against Nicomède. We may already suspect, however, that she is being too clever by half.

The opening scene of Act II reinforces our impression of a beleaguered hero facing long odds. This scene once again portrays sinister villainy with a slightly caricatural edge. Araspe sets out to poison the King's mind against his son, whilst maintaining a façade of impartiality and even of esteem for the prince. His rhetoric adopts a regular pattern of insinuation — 'tout autre que lui' — followed by a disclaimer in which he insists on the perfect *vertu* of Nicomède. Indeed, it is literally true that if the hero did not possess this loyalty, he would pose a dire threat to Prusias. To support his case, Araspe propounds some crudely cynical maxims (433-36), which happen to form an apt comment on Prusias's suspicious mind; while priding himself on his political acumen (373, 455), he lets his panicky imagination run riot (408-10). We now see that the real justification for this scene lies in the excellent preparation it provides for the encounters that are to follow.

Prusias, face to face with his son, moves straight to the offensive: 'Vous voilà, Prince! et qui vous a mandé?' Nicomède disguises the real motives of his journey behind a smoke-screen of filial respect, and we may well speculate on the degree of irony in his declarations, and in Prusias's apparent words of forgiveness that follow. The King appears to recall Araspe's insinuations ('tout autre que vous', 479), and now he seems to justify Nicomède with what had only just now been the burden of his complaint (498-500). It is therefore quite possible that the King's real aim in appointing Nicomède his spokesman is to embroil him with the Romans. Thus the scene is set for the first major confrontation of the play (II, 3).

In opening a scene notable for its bluntness, Flaminius comes straight to the point: Rome has instructed Attale in 'l'art de bien régner' and the envoy demands that he be found a kingdom to rule over. Prusias, with a few words of praise for his elder son, 'passes the buck' to Nicomède. A moment's hesitation, and our hero is on the attack (557 ff.), causing his father to utter a memorable line, as good for a laugh as any in the play: 'Ah! ne me brouillez point avec la République' (564). Flaminius replies with a sneering reference to the effects of Hannibal's tutorship on Nicomède, who, summoned to come to the point by Prusias (has he not done so already?), launches into a sarcastic tirade at his brother's expense:

> Attale a le coeur grand, l'esprit grand, l'âme grande
> Et toutes les grandeurs dont se fait un grand roi. (592-93)

Such undignified cacophonies scandalised Voltaire, who reported that in his own day these lines were 'corrected'. Let Attale prove his worth by leading an army into battle, says Nicomède, offering to serve under him; but Flaminius promises 'd'effroyables tempêtes' (612) from Rome, if such things come to pass. More threats and taunts from both sides, and Nicomède is seething with outraged pride; Prusias is reduced to apologising feebly to Flaminius for his son's unruly behaviour. Soon the envoy, changing tack, puts the proposal to Prusias for the marriage of Attale to Laodice (706-08); Nicomède at once counters by demanding that she be treated like the sovereign she is, with final power of decision (719). He is absolutely right, but is he 'sans intérêt' (713)? Only his swift but defiant withdrawal averts a head-on collision (which, as in *Rodogune*, must not be produced too soon). In their brief final exchange (Scene 4), Prusias seems more optimistic about the outcome than Flaminius, no doubt because he is prepared to use force if necessary. The threat, at the end of Act II, is now concentrated on Laodice.

In Act III, Scene 1, Prusias carries out his undertaking (743) to 'introduce' Flaminius to Laodice; what is more, he tries to force her hand with veiled threats. Laodice responds with irony and diplomatic excuses (757-74). Losing patience, the King resorts to more open threats, though at first he echoes Laodice's words with polite ironies (775-80). In the face of his blustering, she maintains a calm front of offended dignity, based on her confidence in Nicomède. These contrasting attitudes form yet another bout of shadow-boxing, but the reality behind the shadows is beginning to emerge.

In Scene 2, Flaminius addresses Laodice, resisting her demand that he should exit behind Prusias. The ensuing dialogue is a fine example of seventeenth-century rhetoric, of the art of marshalling the most telling arguments, of adapting them to the needs of the immediate situation, and of couching them in persuasive language. The tone is completely serious here despite the persistent presence of irony; history and politics serve to reinforce the conflict of personalities. Flaminius finally comes to the point: Laodice is powerless, virtually a prisoner, at the court of Prusias (829). Her reply consists of a point-by-point rebuttal of Flaminius's arguments, echoing his lines in order to refute them (e.g. 845-46/817-18). Her confidence is based on two factors: Prusias's army is commanded by Nicomède, and she has faith in public opinion (a first hint of the uprising in Act V). The debate then focuses on the question of Roman imperialism. To Flaminius who proclaims that no king is safe today without Roman support (877-78), Laodice replies cuttingly: 'Tous les rois ne sont rois qu'autant qu'il vous plaît' (886). Clearly Flaminius's logic cuts no more ice with Laodice than does Prusias's blackmail. His further reference to the supremacy of Roman arms is countered by a renewed expression of faith in the disciple of Hannibal (909-21), a kind of verbal fanfare which heralds Nicomède's return to the stage (III, 3). This he effects with a comic insolence that shocked Voltaire; Nicomède is implying (927-28, 931-36) that Flaminius's prolonged attentions to Laodice may be more gallant than political. Anger has now got the better of Nicomède, who becomes downright insulting (941). When the envoy indignantly withdraws (III, 4), he at once announces gleefully that Prusias is at this moment interrogating Arsinoé's agents, Métrobate and Zénon, and will soon be enlightened. His optimism is challenged by Laodice's feminine intuition. Why, she asks, is Arsinoé so cocksure? How can they trust the doting Prusias? Attale's arrival produces a brief transition scene (III, 5) in which Laodice withdraws, condemning his importunity. Nicomède, however, will not allow his brother to do likewise (III, 6); he reproaches him with having ignored his earlier demand for a fair and equal contest for the hand of Laodice (1008-12; cf. 266-76). Attale this time makes an adroit reply, which pleases Nicomède, but at this point, there is another interruption — events follow each other swiftly in the second half of Act III — when Araspe informs Nicomède of a summons to appear before the King (III, 7). His peremptory manner (1058) suggests that Nicomède is about to be arrested. Arsinoé follows close behind; her unmotivated entry serves to provide a dialogue in the traditional form of 'stichomythia', with parodical echoes from one line to another. Here she takes mischievous pleasure in teasing Nicomède. Left on-stage with her son (III, 8), Arsinoé drops the mask at once: 'Nous triomphons, Attale...', and proceeds to give him a false account of the affair of the false witnesses. But Attale is no longer such easy game. He perceives Arsinoé's self-interest (1082), instinctively trusts his brother and suspects the felons (1089). In the course of Act III, the spotlight has moved from Laodice to Attale, whose key role in the later stages of the action is being subtly prepared.

With Act IV, our attention is redirected to the plot against Nicomède, who is summoned by Prusias in the first line. Why he needs to be interrogated a second time is not clear, except of course for the audience's benefit. As Scene 1 opens, Arsinoé is besieging Prusias with protestations of innocence. She need hardly bother; the doting Prusias is won over in advance. There follows the essential confrontation between Nicomède and Arsinoé (IV, 2). Nicomède's main line of self-defence is straightforward; in contrast, Arsinoé's initial accusation and her reply are complex and subtle, with plenty of facile emotionalism intended for Prusias, but also much irony: all Nicomède's alleged resentments are put down to jealousy. The success of her oratory is proved by Prusias's fierce question to Nicomède: 'Ingrat! que peux-tu dire?' (1203: the King will maintain his contemptuous use of 'tu' to Nicomède until their final reconciliation, 1818).

Nicomède returns irony for irony, and astutely goes over to the offensive, demanding the death penalty for the two 'double agents' (1215-32). Arsinoé's vehement protests are unnecessary, for Prusias remains rooted in his error, harshly ordering Nicomède: 'Purge-toi d'un forfait si honteux et si bas' (1241). The prince reacts with fierce aristocratic pride: can Prusias really believe that 'un homme de ma sorte' (1243) would commit such paltry crimes? No, if he was disloyal, his offence would be nothing short of insurrection! (1247-54). Nicomède now challenges Arsinoé to say why the villains should not die (1257-66). Does she fear that their last confession will be the truest? With her back to the wall, Arsinoé resorts again to emotional blackmail of Prusias. She asks only that Attale be sent back to Rome; as for herself, she is safe because she will not survive the hour of Prusias's death (1279-84). (She wants to make him panic, to feel that he has to choose now between herself and Nicomède. Her villain's act is so transparent that it required only a moderate carica-ture by Molière to produce Béline's antics in Act I, Scene 7 of *Le Malade imaginaire*.) She then withdraws in apparent distress, but no doubt to summon reinforcements in the person of Flaminius.

Prusias now speaks, and the tone changes at once (IV, 3). After the sustained dramatic tension, his words produce something approaching comic bathos: 'Nicomède, en deux mots, ce désordre me fâche' (1307). The affable but weary tone, the desire for peace and quiet, give Prusias a distinctly un-tragic air. When he expresses his will to be 'mari et père dans cette conjoncture' (1316), Nicomède utters one of those abrupt dramatic repartees for which Corneille had become famous: '—Ne soyez ni l'un ni l'autre. —Et que dois-je être? —Roi' (1318). Then he spells out in uncompromising terms the duty of a monarch to preserve his authority intact (1319-22). Stung by these rebukes, Prusias flies to the opposite extreme:

Choisis, ou Laodice, ou mes quatre couronnes. (1328)

Je ne suis plus ton père, obéis à ton Roi. (1330)

Nicomède stands his ground; this curious scene, which began with a show of false affability, has turned into a no-holds-barred confrontation. The King's defiant words are interrupted by the arrival of Flaminius, accompanied by Attale (who must hear Nicomède's last words, and who is needed for the final two scenes of Act IV).

Act IV, Scene 4, despite its brevity, is one of the most eventful in the play, and as brutal as the previous one. Prusias's fury is apparently unabated; he proclaims that Attale is to be crowned King of Pontus (one of Nicomède's conquests — see 699) and will become his father's sole heir; and also that Nicomède is to be sent to Rome. This he no doubt sees as a convenient way of ridding himself of the rebellious prince, without having him imprisoned or assassinated. Nicomède can only put on a brave face, and resort to wishful thinking; but his words serve to prepare future events (1388-90).

So Attale is now left with Flaminius, to make his own discovery of the realities of Roman 'protection' (IV, 5), summed up in the line: 'Rome ne m'aime pas: elle hait Nicomède' (1456). In reply, Flaminius, deliberately echoing Prusias's recent words (1465; cf. 1394), condemns Attale's ingratitude, reminding him that he depends entirely on Roman patronage. So he is left alone on stage, to deliver the play's only monologue, in which self-interested and idealistic motives are nicely balanced. Attale clearly intends to assist his brother, but how? Yet another act is thus concluded on a note of suspense.

During the interval, an uprising breaks out. Voltaire dismissed this as a 'machine...triviale', but it is not unprepared (see lines 115-16, 450-51, 847-54, 1388-89), and Corneille's first audiences would not have found it implausible (see above, pp.51-52). Arsinoé does not appear excessively concerned by the riots; she is more incensed by Attale's refusal to give up Laodice (1483-84). She uses various arguments to persuade him; but in a resounding tirade charged with irony, he denounces Roman policies, indicating however that he will bow before the storm; Arsinoé lauds his prudence, and continues to do so in the presence of Flaminius (V, 2). The Roman however is more concerned with the threat of the uprising, and urges Arsinoé to react with vigour. Events now follow at top speed: Corneille held that the rules of *vraisemblance* could be relaxed at the dramatic climax to enable this to happen (2, pp.73-74; 8, p.150). Prusias now arrives post-haste (V, 3), with the news that 'les gens de Laodice' are master-minding the operations. Cléone adds to the consternation with her report (V, 4) that Métrobate and Zénon have been lynched by the mob, which is clamouring for Nicomède (1564). Arsinoé still seems curiously unimpressed. Maybe she has foreseen Prusias's violent reaction when Araspe tells him (V, 5) that he cannot vouch much longer for the safe custody of the Prince: 'Sur ses nouveaux sujets faisons voler sa tête' (1588). Attale pleads with him to see reason, while Flaminius characteristically asserts that Nicomède is now untouchable, being Roman property (1599-1605). For his part, the ambassador is ready to escape by a secret route. Arsinoé there-upon announces a 'heaven-sent' solution (1615): let Flaminius take Nicomède with him to the ship, and they will keep the mob at bay with false news until he is safely beyond their reach. The next scene (V, 6) has been much criticised: it is an extended verbal duel between the two female leads, of the kind that Corneille brought off very successfully, but it would be more appreciated if placed at a less urgent moment of the plot. It serves to grant Attale a semblance of the minimum time required to carry out his 'stratagème' (1651). At once Laodice's magnanimity is put to the test. When Arsinoé convinces her that Nicomède is already at sea in a Roman galley, her fury knows no bounds (1720 ff.); but it subsides with almost comical abruptness (1743-44) as soon as the breathless Attale brings the news of Nicomède's escape (V, 7). Attale tells of the 'mysterious' death of Araspe — he does not yet reveal his own part in this — provoking the flight of Nicomède's escort and liberating the Prince. Furthermore, we are told, the panic-stricken Prusias has set sail to join the Romans. But no — hardly are the words uttered when the great monarch himself appears (V, 8), accompanied by Flaminius, in self-congratulatory mood (1765-66). No explanation is offered of their sudden return.

The despairing Arsinoé now urges Prusias to choose suicide rather than a dishonourable death, but Laodice, incensed by this doubt cast on her hero's *générosité*, protests (1771 ff.). Her words form a fitting cue for Nicomède's own entrance (V, 9). His announcement: 'tout est calme' (1779) has a ring of the miraculous about it. His aim, he declares, is to restore legitimate authority in Bithynia, and he urges Prusias and Arsinoé to pardon their rebellious subjects for their zeal in a cause they believed just (1793-96). There is no reason to doubt his sincerity, despite some exaggeration (1798) and an unfortunate echo evoked by the word *bontés* (cf. 1204). Nicomède's magnanimity is in fact less unexpected than Arsinoé's immediate response to it (1811). As she now emerges, the cynical queen is not devoid of grandeur. The psychological process at work here will be familiar to students of Corneille: it is a 'conversion' both intellectual and emotional in character, based on 'admiration' for exceptional *générosité*. This is the process that brings about the denouement not only of this play, but also of *Cinna* (the original model), *Polyeucte* (for those who ignore the supernatural dimension), *Pertharite*, *Agésilas* and *Tite et Bérénice*.

Prusias now takes his cue as usual from Arsinoé (1815-16), and Attale, in the final and rather hackneyed *romanesque* twist to the plot, identifies himself as the mysterious rescuer (1820). Nicomède now attempts to make his peace with Rome, offering friendship to Flaminius, but on terms of strict equality (1843); the Roman's response is admiring but necessarily non-committal (1849-50). Prusias, as incorrigible as any of Molière's heroes, concludes the play with one last repeat of his refrain 'l'amitié des Romains' (1854).

Needless to say, the dénouement of *Nicomède* has proved highly controversial. Corneille admits in his *Examen* that apart from the improbably rapid succession of events (which he plainly does not regard as a major or avoidable defect), his chosen conclusion involves 'quelque inégalité de moeurs', that is, some inconsistency of character. However, this refers only to the unexplained decision of Prusias and Flaminius to abandon their attempt at flight and to return to defend Arsinoé. For modern audiences, however, there would seem to be an equally serious problem of *vraisemblance*, if not about Nicomède's final magnanimity, then at least about his main adversary's reaction to it. Since Arsinoé in particular has established herself as a hardened schemer, it might seem more likely that she is dissimulating to the end, and will take the next opportunity to turn the tables on Nicomède. Such an interpretation was surely not intended by Corneille, though one would not condemn out of hand a stage production that suggested it.

It might also be argued that the ending of *Nicomède* is not quite as miraculous as it at first seems. The hero voluntarily retains his role as heir apparent; he is not even officially rewarded with the hand of Laodice, who stays curiously silent throughout the closing scene. His reputation remains untarnished, but this is only because others have done the inevitable dirty work for him. Rome's response to Nicomède's proposal is unlikely to be positive. Of course, many a theatrical 'happy ending' may appear questionable on reflection; but the question is, how far into the future are we invited to look? Nicomède's triumph may seem fragile, but it was not Corneille's intention that our minds should dwell on its fragility.

Taken as a whole, the action of *Nicomède* forms an outstanding illustration of Corneille's mature dramatic technique. Compared with the 'tetralogy', it is lacking — even more than *Rodogune* — in psychological conflict within the characters. The play's essential content is found in its numerous verbal duels, and in the clash of the personalities involved. There is also, of course, a 'plot' in a quite literal sense, consisting of the actions undertaken against Nicomède by Arsinoé, and his various countermoves. Each act of the play except the third is constructed around one major scene or group of scenes (I, 5; II, 3; IV, 2-4; V, 9), and each except the last ends on an unresolved question giving rise to suspense. In Act III, the dramatic 'weight' is more evenly distributed throughout the eight scenes: the focus is first on Laodice, then it moves via Nicomède to Attale. The total number of scenes in the play is quite high (32), indicating a lot of movement on and off stage; but it is Act V that contains most of the 'real action', in the ordinary sense of palpable events. The denouement brings with it several surprises, but the author has tried to lessen their impact by providing a number of anticipatory passages.

One striking difference between our two plays lies in the relative importance of monologues: exceptional in *Rodogune*, minimal in *Nicomède*. Apart from changing fashion, this is due

above all to the fact that the characters are less isolated in *Nicomède*;
all of them can entrust their secrets to at least one person other than a
confidant. Only Attale experiences, briefly, the kind of mental
conflict that can best be dramatised in monologue form. The near-
absence of monologue also contributes to the much lower rhetorical
'pitch' of *Nicomède*, to its lack of *pompe*.

The unities, in *Nicomède*, no longer present Corneille with the
problems he faced, and solved, earlier in his career. The various
elements of the plot are impeccably integrated. The events portrayed
could plausibly be accomplished in some twelve hours, say from
midday to midnight.[12] Nicomède is on the briefest of visits to court,
Flaminius has a ship at the ready, and in the insurrectional situation
of Act V, events are bound to follow rapidly. As for unity of place,
the action is confined without difficulty to the royal palace; everything that happens outside is reported. However, it demands the
same kind of latitude as *Rodogune*: realistically, the minimum
requirement is a throne-room or audience-chamber for Prusias, plus
a separate apartment for Laodice. In short, the techniques and
conventions we associate with French Classical tragedy are
displayed to perfection in *Nicomède*.[13] The only controversial unity,
so far as this play is concerned, is the fourth one that is sometimes
added to the basic three, that is unity of tone. Here there are some
problems that merit our attention.

### iv) Really a Tragi-Comedy?

The status of *Nicomède* as tragedy has often been questioned.
According to Voltaire, when the play was revived in 1756, it was
billed as a tragi-comedy — a description already found on the title-
page of the first English translation of 1671. It has affinities with its

---

[12]Night has fallen at the beginning of Act V: see line 1481.
[13]This point is well put by R.C. Knight in *6*, p.29: 'The art of squaring a plot
with the requirements of *vraisemblance* and of the unities in particular, of
creating suspense and producing climaxes, of leading by logical steps to a
surprising end, of managing a story of danger and daring and yet subor-
dinating it to a drama of passions and purposes, was never carried further.'

immediate predecessor, *Don Sanche d'Aragon*, which Corneille himself classified as a *comédie héroïque*. However the author (in his *Epître* to *Don Sanche*) gives one clear reason for not putting *Nicomède* in the same category, when he writes that this play is 'une véritable comédie [...] puisqu'on n'y voit naître aucun péril par qui nous puissions être portés à la pitié ou à la crainte'. This, as we have seen, could not be said of *Nicomède*. One could argue also that the hero has no great sacrifices to perform, nor any deep inner conflicts to suffer; but these were not Corneille's criteria. More recent critical judgement has tended to hinge on questions of style and tone, rather than on the nature of the action. Already, Voltaire's commentary on this play shows exasperation at the absence of that solemnity of diction that he always associated with tragedy. (See e.g. his comments on lines 92, 202-04, 339, 592-93, 927-28, 941-42, 1307.) Throughout the stage history of *Nicomède*, performers and producers have commented on this feature. The actor Lekain said of the title role: 'Il faut un grand art [...] pour ne pas y laisser apercevoir le ton de la comédie' (*42*, p.100; *14*, pp.260-64).

There is indeed a considerable range of style in *Nicomède*. Of many apparently comic lines, some are amusing in relation to the character who utters them, usually Prusias (e.g. 564, 1327). Others uttered by Nicomède are so loaded with sarcasm or with sheer impertinence that they come close to burlesque (e.g. 592-93, 927-28). The language used sometimes has a down-to-earth quality which is due to its closeness to the spoken idiom in imagery or syntax (e.g. 92, 547, 1637). Although the total number of such 'irregularities' remains relatively small, there are enough of them to suggest a deliberate move away from the *pompe* of *Rodogune*.

Furthermore, it is not just isolated features of language, but the tone of whole scenes which tends to suggest the style of comedy or tragi-comedy. This is the case already in the second scene of the play, in which Nicomède's incognito is entertainingly exploited. Laodice joins in the taunting of Attale, who becomes something of a 'tête de Turc', with his dignity seriously at risk. In Act III, Scene 7, Arsinoé exploits with mischievous self-satisfaction Nicomède's ignorance of the 'double-cross' to which he has fallen victim. In Act

V, Scene 6, Corneille 'fills in time' with a similar exchange of
*picoteries* between Arsinoé and Laodice. Also worthy of mention are
the first two scenes of Act IV, in which Arsinoé besieges Prusias
with protestations of innocence and devotion. Clearly Corneille did
not intend this to be performed in a caricatural manner, but there are
some moments which are not far removed from Molière, who
caricatured this episode in *Le Malade imaginaire* (I, 7). In addition,
when Prusias, duped by the Queen's antics, attacks Nicomède with
his fierce question: 'Ingrat, que peux-tu dire?' (1203), he momentarily resembles Orgon accusing Damis at the instigation of Tartuffe
(*Tartuffe*, III, 6, 1114). Prusias is the pusillanimous monarch in a
world of *généreux* heroes. Certain lines he utters resemble Molière's
celebrated 'mots de nature', comic either because of their ironical
relevance to the person speaking, or because they sum up an obsession. A good example is Prusias's reproachful question to Nicomède:
'Quelle fureur t'aveugle en faveur d'une femme?' (1340; cf. 1327,
1853-54). But Prusias is definitely not to be seen as a buffoon, rather
as a basically 'anti-*généreux*' ruler with some amusing foibles. Likewise it would be an exaggeration to call Nicomède the jester of the
play, but he does have a talent for entertaining satire. When his anger
is aroused, he is capable of fierce invective (e.g. 951-54); but more
often he prefers to show contempt with a subtler weapon: irony.
Although frequent in Corneille, this is acknowledged to be the
speciality of Nicomède as a character, and of this play in general.
This is not irony of the involuntary, 'Sophoclean' brand; it is deliberate and calculated, implying a different, usually opposite, meaning
from that of the words actually used. Irony is a highly intellectual
mode of expression, which destroys or at least conceals emotion. It
enables Nicomède to jest, to cast ridicule, even to insult, without
appearing flippant or irresponsible (except when he overdoes it, e.g.
592-93). It permits rapid changes of tone, for it can modulate
without warning into deadly seriousness or vehement anger. In
Corneille, it is expressive of *gloire*, in the sense of pride, if not
always of *générosité*; it often gives an impression of contemptuous
superiority. In fact, in the state of passivity to which the hero finds

himself progressively reduced, it is about the only weapon he has left.

Nicomède also uses irony because he enjoys it. This is already obvious in the broadside that he directs at Attale from behind his mask of anonymity (156-82). His reference to a 'défaut de naissance' in the son of the King of Bithynia (176) is a particularly choice specimen. Equally barbed is his ironical comment on Arsinoé's onslaught on him in Act I, Scene 2: 'Que la Reine a pour moi des bontés que j'admire' (1204). The danger with irony lies in the impression of sneering superiority that it can easily convey. The audience may be forgiven for feeling at times that the most intense form of 'admiration' (in the ordinary sense of this term) to be found in this play is that of the hero for himself.

Another aspect of irony in *Nicomède*, as several commentators have pointed out (e.g. 6, pp.24-25), is its infectious nature. In some scenes noted for their comic potential, whether Nicomède is present (III, 7) or not (V, 6), the use of irony takes on the form of tongue-in-cheek exchanges of courtesies. These are Arsinoé's speciality, as she shows early in the play (255-61). The other characters, too, achieve their own particular nuance in the handling of irony. Laodice demonstrates her independence of Prusias with the exaggerated humility of her promises of obedience (750-54). He is of course not deceived, and in reply he also uses irony, in a weakly menacing manner. Arsinoé too employs a more insistent and heavy-handed brand of irony in her main encounter with Nicomède (IV, 2). Flaminius prefers the sneering sort (665-68, 1387), whilst Attale uses it to deceive (1561) or to express his disillusionment with Rome (1511 ff.). Finally, let us not forget Araspe's repeated ironies concerning Nicomède's *vertu* (II, 1).

The effect of irony is sometimes reinforced by one of Corneille's favourite stylistic devices, namely repetition. In scenes of verbal sparring, the deliberate echoing of one character's terms by another can produce an effect of mockery (e.g. 636/637; 666/713; 773-74/775-78; 817-18/845-46; 938/946; 1056/1064; 1058/1066). Sometimes the repetition is delayed, and may therefore be fortuitous; it must be, in cases where the speaker has not been present to hear the words he 'repeats' (e.g. 150/740; 914/1297; 63-64/1411-12. Cf.6, p.24).

So far we have looked for 'tragi-comedy' in *Nicomède* mainly in the field of diction; but the distinctive features of this genre are to be found above all in the plot itself, in the situations it presents, and in the emotions it gives rise to. In *Nicomède*, the dashing young hero, though short of opportunities to prove his physical prowess, exhibits all the conventional perfections of a *héros de roman*, including a highly developed sense of 'fair play'. He is persecuted in a somewhat 'cloak-and-dagger' manner by villains who are sometimes a little too transparently villainous, and is rescued by a half-brother, whom he ultimately recognises thanks to a stock novelistic device (the ring). These plot details were all invented by Corneille. However, the plot does not depend on any devices such as mistaken or concealed identity, as was the case in the majority of tragi-comedies. The *romanesque* (or melodramatic) content of *Nicomède* appears unremarkable, when compared even to that of *Rodogune*. This is just as true of the role of love. The undoubted mutual attachment between Nicomède and Laodice is not developed. The first lines of the play, embodying the conventional conceit of *le vainqueur vaincu*, pay homage once and for all to the emotional ties of this unemotional couple, after which we are left to take them for granted.

The other feature that appears to link *Nicomède* with tragi-comedy is the 'happy ending'; but Corneille had already adopted this in a number of his tragedies. He thereby introduced a Christian dimension, implying rejection of the notion of tragic Fate and its replacement by a kindly Providence. This assumed the capacity of man's free will, enlightened by reason, to overcome the baser passions, notably vengeance. In the political sphere, it implied that no problem of statecraft is insoluble, if the magnanimous ruler shows moderation and clemency, the example of which will challenge every *généreux* to do likewise. In the optimistic perspective of Christian heroic drama, problems such as the rivalry of king and hero, or the clash between the aristocratic ethic of *générosité* and Machiavellian realism in politics, no longer appeared intractable.

However, nearly all Corneille's tragedies retained two features that were never shared by tragi-comedy: their essentially historical and political orientation, and the fairly rigorous logic of their characters' motivation.

## *v) The Characters*

No work of Corneille is more accomplished than *Nicomède* in its characterisation, with six effectively individualised personages, plus a confidant who is more than a mere cipher. These individuals form a pattern of complements and contrasts, the symmetry of which is governed by two main axes. There is firstly that of age. The senior generation, consisting of Prusias, Arsinoé and no doubt Flaminius, represents both experience and vested interests. Opposed to them, Nicomède, Laodice and eventually Attale embody the idealism and independence of youth. Secondly, there is the political axis, formed by the characters' contrasting attitudes to Rome.

If Nicomède does not quite compare as a hero to Rodrigue, Horace, Auguste or Polyeucte, it is no doubt because he experiences neither suffering nor inner conflict. He never questions the line of conduct that he instinctively adopts. As Corneille created him, he owes nothing to history except the name of Nicomède and his status as son of Prusias II of Bithynia. His personality is therefore the result of a very deliberate choice on the author's part, and its unity suggests an exemplary quality. 'Nicomède n'est-il pas dans l'ordre du bien ce que Cléopâtre de Syrie est dans l'ordre du mal?' asks one critic (*32*, pp.178-79). His character traits are established beyond dispute, but there is dissension about their origin and their significance. In Couton's opinion (*12*, pp.62-72) Nicomède represents the Prince de Condé as seen by his many supporters in early 1651 — a general whose military genius was matched by his loyalty to the Queen Regent, despite her harsh treatment of him. Recently, however, André Georges (*32*) has questioned Couton's analogies in order to present a very different theory, namely that Nicomède is the 'magnanimous man' as portrayed in Aristotle's *Nicomachean Ethics*, Book V — a text which our author, like most educated men of his time, undoubtedly knew well. Both Nicomède and Aristotle's exemplar are courageous and ardent in their quest for fame; they are also loyal, disinterested and averse to trickery, to the point of sometimes appearing naïve or disdainful. However, this represents in broad terms an ideal of aristocratic conduct recommended by many moralists of Corneille's day, and recognised if not always practised by many a nobleman who had never read a line of Aristotle.

As statements about one of the play's principal sources, these two theories are mutually exclusive, yet they both suggest that Nicomède is an exemplary figure, a spokesman for a set of heroic values. What his character appears to symbolise is the contemporary ideal of *générosité* placed in the service of an ideal of royal sovereignty. He is determined to show Prusias how a true king should comport himself. But Nicomède is a soldier and an idealist, rather than a practical politician. He is straightforward and trusting to a fault (like Antiochus) and consequently vulnerable to the ruses of unscrupulous politicians. It was something of a seventeenth-century commonplace to portray the disinterested *généreux* as easy prey for the wily court practitioners of 'la politique intéressée'.

Another of his political faults is impulsiveness, both in word and deed. Loyalty to Prusias will not curb his razor-sharp tongue (624-26), nor will any fear of provoking a 'diplomatic incident' deter his insolence to Flaminius. Is this just the impulsiveness of youth, as Prusias explains to the Roman envoy? How old is Nicomède then? We learn that he has commanded an army for ten years, which even if he is as precocious a military genius as Condé himself was, must put him well into his thirties. His fiercest outbursts are reserved for the Romans and their collaborators, including Attale, to whom he speaks with equal sharpness (III, 6). His reply to Arsinoé's charge of base intrigue is symptomatic of this slightly contemptuous attitude:

> Vous ne savez que trop qu'un homme de ma sorte,
> Quand il se rend coupable, un peu plus haut se porte,
> Qu'il lui faut un grand crime à tenter son devoir,
> Où sa gloire se sauve à l'ombre du pouvoir. (1243-46)

Such pride should be seen not as overweening vanity, but as a seventeenth-century nobleman's belief in the excellence conferred on him by his rank. This involves keeping up certain appearances. Nicomède's fearlessness includes an element of gamesmanship, of bluff. Never to appear daunted is a rule of the game, and only once does Nicomède fail to obey it, when he momentarily reels under the blow of being condemned to exile in Rome (1383 ff.).

In the end, the hero's exemplary *générosité* is proved by his supreme act of clemency, which is essentially a gesture of trust. Up to this point, he may perhaps be dubbed a hero in word rather than deed, preferring proud declarations and verbal fencing to decisive action. Corneille, however, intended with his final scene to leave no doubt about Nicomède's heroic status, nor about the calculated audience-response:

> Ce héros de ma façon sort un peu des règles de la tragédie, en ce qu'il ne cherche point à faire pitié par l'excès de ses infortunes; mais le succès a montré que la fermeté des grands coeurs, qui n'excite que de l'admiration dans l'âme du spectateur, est quelquefois aussi agréable que la compassion, que notre art nous ordonne d'y produire par la représentation de leurs malheurs. (*8*, p.150)

As for the idea of *admiration*, it is clear that, in the case of Nicomède if not of Cléopâtre, Corneille counts on our moral approval as well as on our astonishment.

As many critics have remarked and sometimes complained, the character of Laodice is the mirror image of Nicomède, his feminine counterpart. Laodice exhibits the same qualities as her hero: the same pluck, rising in moments of adversity to quixotic self-confidence (1725-31); the same scornfully ironical turns of phrase (885 ff.) and the same legalistic turn of mind (1689 ff.); the same views of kingship (894 ff.) and on magnanimous clemency (1664-66, 1771-75). There is never a hint of a rift between them. Complaints of monotony in Corneille's presentation of this heroic couple are therefore understandable. At the most Laodice shows a few minor distinguishing traits: her feminine intuition (985 ff.), her capacity for passionate anger which threatens to undermine her *générosité* (1720-24), and her greater initiative and resourcefulness, as demonstrated in Act V (but this is also due to a difference of situation: she does not owe the same allegiance to Prusias as does Nicomède).[14] Their relationship raises no problems until the end of the play, when its future remains enveloped in mystery. Surprisingly, Laodice does not utter a word in the final scene, nor does Nicomède address one to her. The question of their marriage is not broached again; indeed, it seems to be carefully avoided. Is this not the one reward that Nicomède could legitimately have asked for? He is surely now in a position to obtain it without difficulty. Perhaps Corneille shied away from a plot invention that would logically have had consequences far beyond the scope of the play: the marriage would have represented a major defeat for Roman diplomacy (cf. *43*, pp.498-99; *22*, pp.106-07). Yet Corneille's adherence to history in *Nicomède* is so minimal that one wonders why he declined to add this embellishment to his 'happy ending'.

Attale is a rather more important and interesting character than may appear at first glance. He is one of a limited number of characters in French classical tragedy — limited because of the effect of unity of time — who change decisively in the course of the action. As a result, he suffers genuine inner conflict, though it is not given anything like the prominence that Corneille would have accorded it at an earlier stage in his career.

Even in the early scenes, Attale does not appear odious, but he is not particularly admirable either — a pampered young prince with little initiative of his own, petulant but ever inclined to retreat behind the might of Rome and the authority of his father (145-54). If not obviously *généreux*, he is proud: he woos Laodice above all to avoid

---

[14] Her father appointed Prusias her guardian (59-60), but her present status at the court of Bithynia is unclear. Has a palace revolution deprived her of her throne in Armenia? Nicomède talks of restoring her power by force of arms (517-19). At present she seems to be enjoying (?) 'une captivité dorée dans une cour étrangère', according to A. Stegmann, *21*,II, p.368.

the 'affront' of remaining subordinate to Nicomède (222). He is quick to recognise and admire his brother's magnanimity; indeed, from the viewpoint of strict *vraisemblance*, Attale may appear over-eager to place his trust so completely in a man he hardly knows except by reputation. But one of the play's axioms is that *générosité* implies trust; another, that it is both easy to recognise and infectious. Attale appears shamed by his brother's disdainfully harsh words (1033), for almost at once he shows signs of a change of heart in his spirited reply to his mother's calumny of Nicomède (III, 8). Soon, however, comes a relapse, for on being promised the throne, Attale assumes that Laodice will now be his (1419-21). It is Flaminius's reluctance on this subject, and what it reveals of Rome's policies, that proves to be the decisive factor. Various motives may be at work here. Does Attale act out of pique, at not getting his expected reward? Or is it a moral revulsion against injustice, combined with recognition of his brother's courage in a just cause? Above all, Attale realises that Rome regards him not as an ally, but as a vassal, even a tool. Ironically, it is the 'virtue' instilled in him by his Roman upbringing that makes him rebel against Roman 'Realpolitik'.

In fact, Attale's personality, though perfectly consistent, has been largely shaped by the needs of the plot. This is basically how French classical drama (and most other drama) works, and we should acknowledge this when we attempt to analyse the 'psychology' involved. What Corneille needed for the later stages of the action was an appropriate instrument of salvation for Nicomède, well-placed and ruthless enough to carry out the unavoidable criminal act, and thus relieve the prince of moral responsibility for it. When the time comes, Attale dissimulates impressively, and having performed the unpleasant task, he is content to withdraw and to allow Nicomède to gather the laurels, in an ultimate skirmish with Rome (1830 ff.).

In contrast to youthful *générosité*, the political self-interest of the older generation often takes on the most unscrupulous forms. In this respect Arsinoé is the most active character, just as she is the protagonist of the plot. She seems proud of her own resourcefulness, and there is (just as in the case of Cléopâtre) a distinctly histrionic side to her manipulations (e.g. 339-42). Her plans are based on psychological calculations about the likely reactions of her victims. The manner in which she despatches Métrobate and Zénon to Nicomède's camp, and the complicated role she devises for them as 'double agents', reveal the subtlety of her double-dealing. She can 'play' Prusias like an expert instrumentalist; this manipulatory art is the secret of her power. Her rhetoric makes use of insinuation as well as persuasion, and she can sense the moment when logical argument needs to be reinforced by emotional blackmail (e.g. 1267 ff.). Her self-confidence in moments of apparent peril reflects her awareness of being one move ahead of her adversaries (e.g. III, 7).

Yet we may have our doubts about Arsinoé. Is not her self-confidence sometimes exaggerated, or misplaced? In her more overtly hypocritical moments, she may be judged too transparently villainous (e.g. 1283 ff.). Critics refer to her unprincipled opportunism, to her 'machiavélisme sans grandeur'. They rightly explain her short-comings by her emotional attachment to Attale, for whom she conceives excessive ambitions: a modest throne in a neighbouring state would no doubt have been a more realistic objective than her brazen attempt to deprive Nicomède of his birthright. What she lacks is a grandeur in crime equal to that of Cléopâtre, though she often rivals the Syrian queen in hypocrisy and mendacity. The difference is that, unlike Cléopâtre, Arsinoé does not include the murder of close relatives among her tactical options. It might have been simpler to hire an assassin to dispose of Nicomède than to weave her elaborate plot; but that would of course have made a less interesting play.

In fact Arsinoé is a formidable adversary; her plot comes within an ace of succeeding, and fails only because she did not foresee such initiative from Attale. She is always resourceful, modifying her tactics to meet an unforeseen reaction or event (V, 1), never at a loss for a stratagem (1615, 1640). It would be foolish to underestimate Arsinoé, even though Corneille chose to depict her as a somewhat unspectacular villain in comparison with Cléopâtre.

It remains true that the real source of Arsinoé's strength lies in her husband's weakness. Prusias is one of Corneille's best-known 'unheroic' characters, who in comparison with the *généreux* must appear contemptible and even slightly comic. Voltaire repeatedly described him as a 'vieillard de comédie'. Exploited by his domineering queen with whom he is infatuated, Prusias evokes distant echoes of the hen-pecked husband and the amorous dotard of ancient farce. His main concern is his own peace of mind, which has to be preserved by pacifying his queen. It is unlikely, however, that in a play subtitled *tragédie*, Corneille aimed to provoke real mirth at Prusias's expense. What he offers us is an in-depth study of a weak but not stupid monarch, whose behaviour runs counter to accepted seventeenth-century norms of kingship. Caught in the cross-fire between the warring factions, Prusias finds it hard to be consistent. He gives way almost automatically to Arsinoé, and to Flaminius as spokesman for Rome; he derives the strength to resist Nicomède only from jealousy, suspicion and the sheer terror aroused in him by his son's anti-Roman zeal. Like other weak rulers, Prusias sees all resistance as an affront to his authority, which leads him to take impulsive or violent decisions (e.g. 1327-30). So long as he has hopes of getting his own way, he can be affable enough (1307 ff.). His basic instinct however is to flee from responsibility or danger, and in the final crisis he briefly abandons even Arsinoé (1760-64).

However, Prusias is not often odious. He even has one or two endearing characteristics which he shares with other Cornelian 'faibles', notably with Félix in *Polyeucte*. With disarming candour, he confides his innermost motives and emotions to his counsellor Araspe, in words distinctly recalling those of Félix (413-30; cf. *Polyeucte*, III, 5, 1004 ff.). Here Prusias reveals his most serious failing: his inability to bear the burden of gratitude placed on him by Nicomède's military victories. His resentment against his son can even inspire him with truly regal language, if he thinks he has a just reproach to deliver (472-80, 504-14). Corneille himself insists that Prusias is not bloodthirsty by nature (*8*, p.38, line 29 and *2*, p.37).

Nor is he a political ignoramus or imbecile. Far from seeking to betray his country, he believes that the Roman alliance is essential for Bithynia. He knows that Rome, now committed to a policy of eastward imperial expansion, cannot tolerate the acquisition by his

strategically important kingdom of virtually the whole of northern
Asia Minor, which is what would happen if to Nicomède's conquests
— Cappadocia (28), Pontus (468) and Galatia (699) — were added
the kingdom of Armenia, through his marriage to Laodice (27,
pp.62-64). From the 'realistic' point of view as expounded by
Arsinoé, Prusias has every reason to fear his son's ambitions, and
finally it is only the hero's magnanimity that preserves his father's
rule. The play therefore dramatises a political choice, ostensibly
between heroism and cowardice, or between *générosité* and
'Machiavellianism'; but the alternatives may just as plausibly be
seen, as they are by Prusias, as realism and temerity. Not many
Nicomèdes have been vindicated by history.[15]

      In Prusias, Corneille presents not only a shrewd if
uncourageous politician, but a complex individual who is sometimes
difficult to pin down. Is he always Arsinoé's dupe? How are we
meant to judge his ultimate volte-face (1765 ff.)? The irony so
prominent in *Nicomède* leaves room here and there for ambiguity
and doubt. For instance, is his insistence that Nicomède should reply
on his behalf to Flaminius (545 ff.) just an attempt to 'pass the buck',
or is it more probably part of a plan to embroil his son with Rome?
Yet he tries to pacify Flaminius (635-36) when the argument
becomes too heated. And is his final explosion of wrath (723)
genuine or feigned? Prusias may well be alarmed, but we can also
imagine him secretly exhilarated at the spectacle of the two men who
most intimidate him at loggerheads. Finally, why does he propose to
deliver Nicomède into Roman hands? Is he exasperated at his son's
defiance? Or has he decided to rid himself of the turbulent prince,
without incurring responsibility for his imprisonment or his assassi-
nation? Such uncertainties give some latitude to the performer, and
also subtlety and depth to a role that may otherwise seem rather
facile.

---

[15] However, Charles de Gaulle was one, and as a result this play gained
particular resonances in the immediate post-war years: see an article by
Robert Kemp written in 1950, quoted from *Le Monde* by R.C. Knight, *6*,
p.30.

Flaminius is important for his function as ambassador rather than for his personality. His presence serves to enlarge the scope of the action, linking personal motives with the wider political issues. In fact, Corneille's confusion between Flaminius and Flamininus, whether conscious or not, serves precisely to present the Roman envoy as doubly motivated: he has a father to avenge as well as Senate instructions to obey. At first, he seems to be Arsinoé's tool, since (according to another of the author's 'historical inventions') Attale has returned from Rome to Bithynia in exchange for the extradition of Hannibal, who as a result has committed suicide; and Flaminius is now pressing Prusias to grant the hand of Laodice to Attale (33-38), according to Arsinoé's plan, of which he is not fully informed.

Whatever his human failings, Flaminius is an exemplary ambassador. He wraps up the Senate's harsh demands in suitably diplomatic terms, showing the proverbial iron fist beneath the velvet glove. He can skilfully improvise a stalling operation in a situation that is not foreseen in his instructions (IV, 5). He presents his country's policies as 'disinterested', inspired by the official code of *vertu* (in which Attale believes), rather than by national self-interest or *raison d'état* (e.g. 665-88). His eulogies of Roman excellence are not devoid of what we would now call racism: he boasts of Rome's heaven-sent civilising mission, and can barely hide his pity for those unfortunates who have not been born its citizens (680, 901-08, 922-25). Flaminius is also a man of action, insisting on a swift and decisive response to the threat of the uprising (1539 ff., 1571-78), but still mindful of Roman interests when it comes to the choice of means (1599 ff.). The events which bring about the dénouement signify the failure of his mission, but he manages to salvage his own dignity by responding with true *généreux* admiration to Nicomède's magnanimity, but while taking care to say nothing that may compromise Roman interests in any way.

The personality of Araspe serves merely as a comment on the cause he serves. He is the evil counsellor who, by seventeenth-century convention, bears the blame for the misdeeds of a weak monarch, according to the doctrine that 'the King can do no wrong'.

His method is that of sly ironical insinuation (369-72, 397-400, 441-42). He represents Machiavellian politics in its most virulent form. By the same convention, the counsellor becomes the scapegoat: Araspe is the only victim of the uprising among the named cast. His role serves to underline, in its modest way, the fact that in *Nicomède* the characters are not just personalities, but also the representatives of attitudes of mind, of moral and political doctrines and values. This is a point which requires some expansion and clarification.

## vi) Morals, Politics and History

*Nicomède* is one of Corneille's most densely political tragedies. The issues count as much as the personalities, and the ideological debate forms a vital part of the play's meaning. The cut-and-thrust of partisan debate lends the play its characteristic tone, aided by stylistic features such as interrupted dialogue, repetition and irony. As is his custom, Corneille presents every point of view with exhilarating vigour, and even the 'villains' are allowed to make out the best possible case for their villainy (e.g. Flaminius in II, 3, 665 ff.). The characters are granted an abundance of historical examples to quote in discussion (e.g. lines 604-06, 675-78; 1297-1300, 1524, 1547-50). The central theme, according to the author, is Roman colonialism: 'Mon principal but a été de peindre la politique des Romains au dehors, et comme ils agissaient impérieusement avec les Rois leurs alliés...' (8, p.39). The issues raised by Roman policies, as depicted by Corneille, are numerous and complex.

As stated in the passage just quoted, the principal allies (or adversaries, if Nicomède has his way) of the Romans were the monarchs of the ancient world. National independence is identified by Corneille with the defence of royal sovereignty. The King's authority is portrayed here in its seventeenth-century absolutist form, as a consequence of Divine Right. A king, in order to fulfil his divine mission, must achieve mastery over personal attachments, and serve only the interests of his realm. The hero sternly admonishes his father, who is eager to be 'père et mari', that his one legitimate concern is to be 'Roi'. To this, Nicomède immediately adds:

> Un véritable roi n'est ni mari ni père;
> Il regarde son trône, et rien de plus. Régnez,
> Rome vous craindra bien plus que vous ne la craignez...
>
> (1320-22)

Nicomède has been described as providing 'the most memorable defence of Kingship in the entire theatre of Corneille' (*19*, p.175). His insolence to Flaminius is expressive of his belief in the sacred nature of royal sovereignty: Rome's pretension to set up a chain of 'puppet kings' is not only a crime but an absurdity, a contradiction in terms, and merits only scorn (588-91). His vigorous defence of Laodice's prerogatives as Queen of Armenia (714-19, 726) is based on the same convictions, as is his tactical call for the execution of Métrobate and Zénon, guilty of *lèse-majesté* (1215-32). In this respect too, Laodice is the mirror image of Nicomède. She has an equally lofty conception of a monarch's dignity (57-64). Her refugee status, she insists, cannot affect her royal prerogatives, whatever Prusias may threaten (786-89; cf. 757-74). For her too, an obedient monarch is an absurdity (898). This elevated view of monarchy is shared by Attale despite his Roman education (147, 1468) and can even inspire Prusias to eloquence when it suits him (505-14, 1339-42).

For the most part, however, Prusias is depicted as traitor to the cause of kings. He has no firm will of his own; nearly all his actions are reactions to the initiatives of others. He cannot overcome his jealous mistrust of Nicomède (105, 420-24), and is incapable of recognising Nicomède's essential loyalty, for he naturally sees others in his own image (410-12). As a result, Prusias is vulnerable to the insinuations of Arsinoé and Araspe, about the danger presented by his son: 'Qui se lasse d'un roi peut se lasser d'un père' (408). His legitimate royal power has been emptied of real authority; it is a hollow shell which he is tempted to reinforce with tyrannical acts (*20*, pp.291-99). Though not naturally inclined to violence, he will use it if put under sufficient pressure (1588). His betrayal of the ideal of kingship is summed up in the advice he gives to Attale, always to look to Rome for support: it offers a vision of monarchy on crutches (1392-94). Arsinoé also has some cynical thoughts about royal virtue

(1117-18). Clearly the subversion of true monarchical doctrine is well advanced at the court of Prusias, and so Laodice will have little scruple or difficulty in fomenting a revolt in favour of Nicomède. No approval of rebellion is implied, even though Prusias, in attempting to eliminate Nicomède, has violated the basic law of primogeniture. Laodice even brands the rebels she leads as criminals; for unlike her, they are Prusias's subjects (1692-99). In the last scene, Corneille does all he can to restore the prestige of Prusias's throne; this is one of the purposes of the exchange of magnanimities.

Until this near-miraculous moment, however, the crisis appears dangerous in the extreme. It is the climax of a conflict that has been latent in Cornelian drama ever since Rodrigue's dazzling victories in *Le Cid* threatened to eclipse the King, Don Fernand (20). In no other play except his last, *Suréna*, does Corneille dramatise this conflict so comprehensively as he does in *Nicomède*. The danger of a rift between hero and monarch was a vivid reality in contemporary France, with the brilliant general, Condé, on the brink of rebellion, torn personally between the defence of what he considered to be his vital interests, and his duty and reputation as protector of the young Louis XIV. Likewise Nicomède, faced with Hannibal's suicide, the threats against Laodice and the 'revelations' of Arsinoé's agents, sees no choice but to abandon his army in order to confront his father. He offers obedience, but it is no longer unconditional: 'Mais je demande un prix de mon obéissance' (516). His language is no longer that of a submissive subject; he insults the Roman ambassador, and when Prusias tries to restrain him, he becomes defiant: 'Ou laissez-moi parler, Sire, ou faites-moi taire' (624). Not surprisingly, Prusias sees his son's attitude as 'une insolente et fausse obéissance' (395). Through the combined effect of jealousy and perfidious advice, the very existence of the hero is becoming intolerable to the suspicious monarch. Nicomède, as a result, is virtually put on trial; this play, especially Act IV, follows the tendency of Cornelian drama to take on the form of judicial proceedings. The hero is becoming the victim of royal aggression; yet Prusias is no bloodthirsty tyrant, like Phocas in *Héraclius*. He is only 'un faible'; but as Racine so brilliantly demonstrated in *Britannicus*, weakness of character can be as dangerous as malice, when a ruler faces an explosive situation.

The quality Prusias lacks is the very one that Corneille and his age identified with heroism, namely *générosité*. In contrast, Nicomède is the living incarnation of this virtue. This was the main purpose behind the liberties Corneille took with history (*1*, II, p.1461). When he wrote in the *Au lecteur/Examen*, 'La grandeur du courage y règne seul' (*8*, p.38), he implied that the truly royal personage is Nicomède, who dominates through his *générosité*, even if he does not occupy the throne. The words *généreux* and *générosité* are found eleven times altogether in *Nicomède*, with a fairly wide range of meanings, including physical and military bravery (550), disinterestedness (673), independence and self-reliance (1110), above all chivalry and a sense of fair play (960, 1090, 1664, 1722, 1744). The *généreux* will never seize an unfair advantage, slander his adversary or strike him when he is down. Aversion to violence is also implied, as we see from Laodice's threats and their subsequent withdrawal (1722, 1744). Overtones of the Latin *generosus* ('of noble clan') can still be heard in the use of this term. The adjective *magnanime*, also found several times, is synonymous with *généreux* (1271, 1471, 1775, 1848). It refers to high courage and nobility of soul, though it can be used ironically (1271).

Another term prominent in *Nicomède* is *vertu*, which is also quite often used with a meaning close to its etymological sense, namely 'manliness'. It sometimes denotes courage or valour (596, 640, 644, 656), but is more often associated with moral qualities such as loyalty, uprightness, and again a sense of fair play. (See lines 39, 289, 367, 400, 405, 412, 441, 1116, 1118, 1134, 1167, 1830. In some cases, the use of this word is plainly ironical.) In a few instances, *vertu* indicates the heroic quality of magnanimity and sagacity (i.e. *prudence* — 807, 816, 820, 1048). Flaminius is particularly insistent on this idea in the unsolicited advice he gives to Laodice (816-20). These two words, and their range of meanings, are useful pointers to the moral values implicitly acknowledged in *Nicomède*.[16]

The concept of *générosité* can also be defined negatively. Self-interest is its most direct antithesis: the *généreux* must not appear to be motivated by material ambition or by the prospect of personal gain; he must above all appear public-spirited. On hearing Flaminius's proposal that Laodice should marry Attale, Nicomède promises to reply briefly: 'Je n'y réponds qu'un mot, étant sans intérêt' (713). On this occasion, it is difficult to believe him. Flaminius certainly doesn't, for he has just delivered a broadside against Nicomède on this theme (665-680). The main purpose of the dénouement is to enable the hero finally to display a disinterested-ness more genuine than that of any Roman.

Closely allied to the theme of disinterestedness is that of 'fair play', straightforwardness and personal independence. Here 'la générosité' is explicitly opposed to 'la fourbe' (*fourberie* in modern French). True heroism in Corneille — and nowhere more emphatically than in *Nicomède* — is proclaimed to be incompatible with any form of cunning or trickery. The sinister activities of Arsinoé, characterised by 'artifice' (296), are all based on a simple rule of conduct: '...Il n'est ni fourbe ni crime/ Qu'un trône acquis par là ne rende légitime' (291-92). Such revelations can be made only in private, even by Arsinoé. In his *Au lecteur/ Examen*, Corneille states that 'la grandeur du courage' uses but one weapon in its struggle against 'la politique' and its 'artifices': this is 'une prudence généreuse, qui marche à visage découvert' (*8*, p.38). This does not mean that the hero will always be law-abiding, but a Nicomède will instinctively choose open rebellion rather than 'mean tricks', if his aim is to gain power (1242-56). Trickery is rejected as 'le partage des femmes' (1256), but 'virile' heroism, he implies, will always prefer

---

[16] On the other hand, the use of the word *gloire* is unremarkable in *Nicomède*. It is found with the meaning of 'pride', or most often of 'renown'. Occasionally it denotes a more heroic kind of self-respect, or sense of personal distinction (e.g. lines 45, 457, 552). On the use of such 'heroic vocabulary' in Corneille, see *18*, pp.287 ff.

openness to stealth, straightforwardness and single combat to double-dealing. As a major point in his own defence, Nicomède stresses his innocence of all such practices (1160-68), and Attale is won over in advance to his brother's point of view (1107-12). It is this loudly professed belief in 'fair play' that makes Nicomède appear so naïve at times, but according to the code of values implied in the play, such 'innocence' ought to count in his favour (*34*, pp.342-45).

Yet whatever the importance of the political and moral issues in *Nicomède*, according to the author the dominating theme is historical. The crucial passage of the *Au lecteur/ Examen* must now be quoted in full:

> Mon principal but a été de peindre la politique des
> Romains au dehors, et comme ils agissaient impérieuse-
> ment avec les rois leurs alliés, leurs maximes pour les
> empêcher de s'accroître, et les soucis qu'ils prenaient de
> traverser leur grandeur, quand elle commençait à leur
> devenir suspecte à force de s'augmenter et de se rendre
> considérable par de nouvelles conquêtes. (*8*, p.39)

Opinions may differ as to whether this is really the central theme of the play, but there can be no doubt of its prominence. The play's interest thus transcends that of the individual characters, embracing some of the great political issues in the ancient world.

Many among Corneille's audience had been nurtured on the culture and history of ancient Rome, which occupied a far more important place in the contemporary school curriculum than those of France. Rome is given a prominent position in Cornelian drama from *Horace* onwards. (*Rodogune* is one of Corneille's few historical tragedies that makes no mention of Rome.) At first sight, *Nicomède* seems to mark a change of direction. This time, it appears, Rome will not be glorified: the viewpoint will be that of the 'opposition', of the victims, actual and potential, of Rome's ruthless expansionism. Prominent among these at this point in history (c. 150 BC) were the monarchs of Asia Minor. Corneille gives some prominence to the republican tradition of contempt for crowned heads (156-82, 198-

201). To Flaminius, nothing that stands in the path of Roman
territorial ambitions is to be tolerated. He treats both monarchs and
the principles of hereditary monarchy with scorn, virtually ordering
Prusias to appoint Attale his successor in place of Nicomède (540-
42). Attale's bitter discovery is that neither Nicomède nor himself
represents anything for Roman diplomacy but a tool, and a potential
hostage. He angrily condemns Rome's policy of 'divide and rule' in a
passage (1505 ff.) which anticipates a celebrated page of
Montesquieu (see 7, p.110). But for Flaminius it is vital to prevent
the marriage of Nicomède and Laodice, so that a large part of Asia
Minor will not fall into the hands of a potential adversary of Rome.
(A glance at an historical map of this region — e.g. 8, p.41 — will
make this point perfectly clear.) Rome might allow Nicomède to
keep his conquests, but never to acquire Armenia in addition (697-
708); this is why Attale finds himself in trouble in Act IV. Flaminius
speaks with some brutality on this subject, even to Prusias in person
(1599-1605). Such hectoring language turns the ambassador into the
symbol not only of Roman *Realpolitik*, but also of Roman arrogance.
His tactics are effective but highly unscrupulous, being a combination of intimidation and bribery, of aggression and guile.

Yet at the end, the image of Rome emerges relatively
unscathed. The self-interested motive in Flaminius's mission (21 ff.)
does him no personal credit, but it exonerates all the other Romans
from the charge of having pursued to the bitter end their vendetta
against Hannibal. According to Livy (Book XXIX), the Senate itself
ordered Flamininus to demand the surrender of Hannibal by Prusias
I, and this was the direct cause of the Carthaginian's suicide. In
Corneille's version, Arsinoé is allowed to tell a very different story,
incriminating only herself and Flaminius (297-304). For all her
cynicism, she has respect for Roman political *mores*, and so prefers
to hide the more sordid details of her plot from Attale (288-92).
Allies and enemies alike pay homage to Rome, either for its
prestigious might or for its public-spirited ideal of *vertu*. Despite his
barrage of irony, Nicomède in the end exonerates Flaminius (1787-
90), and his very last words, addressed to the ambassador, are devoid
of all his former venom (1839-44). Flaminius's final reply is in the

same vein, though necessarily provisional in its content. So although the play ends with the triumph of Nicomède at the court of Bithynia, the outcome of his struggle with Rome might more accurately be described as a draw, or as 'match postponed'.

## vii) A New Kind of Tragedy?

Corneille tended to see his theatrical career as an ongoing series of experiments. 'Voici une pièce d'une constitution assez extraordinaire' is the opening remark of the *Au lecteur/ Examen* of *Nicomède*. The author evidently regarded it as an unorthodox play, a slightly risky experiment (*8*, p.38). We have examined some of the unorthodox features of *Nicomède*. Its right to the designation *tragédie* is indisputable only if we keep to the purely formal criteria which were those of Corneille's time. Most critics would agree that in this play 'l'art cornélien est en train d'exténuer le tragique' (*18*, p.221). We have noted its lack of inner conflict; neither Nicomède nor Laodice, for instance, is faced with the kind of difficult choice between love and honour or political ambition that used to be the hallmark of Cornelian drama. Except at rare moments, the hero displays a self-confidence and a serenity that we do not associate any more with a tragic protagonist; his optimism is vindicated by the dénouement, which is the supreme expression of Nicomède's faith in human nature. How can we then see him as a victim of tragic fate? The only form of destiny suggested in the play concerns the future hegemony of Rome.

What of the emotions traditionally associated with tragedy since Aristotle, pity and fear? We may well experience some alarm for the safety of Nicomède, as does Laodice; but can he be said to compel our pity (which this latter-day Stoic hero would no doubt reject as a 'weak' emotion)? Corneille made some observations on this subject which are interesting but not totally consistent. The first is the well-known sentence in the first paragraph of the *Au lecteur/ Examen*: 'La tendresse et les passions, qui doivent être l'âme des tragédies, n'ont aucune part en celle-ci: la grandeur du courage y règne seule et regarde son malheur d'un oeil si dédaigneux qu'il n'en

saurait arracher une plainte' (*8*, p.38). Later on in the same text, he
goes on to claim:

> Ce héros de ma façon sort un peu des règles de la
> tragédie, en ce qu'il ne cherche point à faire pitié par
> l'excès de ses malheurs; mais le succès a montré que la
> fermeté des grands coeurs, qui n'excite que de
> l'admiration dans l'âme du spectateur, est quelquefois
> aussi agréable que la compassion que notre art nous
> commande de mendier pour leurs misères. (*8*, pp.39-40)

In this text of 1651, Corneille sounds confident of having added a
new paragraph, as it were, to Aristotle's *Poetics*. However, when
transforming the *Au lecteur* into the 1660 *Examen*, he added,
immediately after the word *misères*: 'Il en fait naître toutefois
quelqu'une [*compassion*], mais elle ne va pas jusques à tirer des
larmes. Son effet se borne à mettre les auditeurs dans les intérêts de
ce prince et à leur faire former des souhaits pour ses prospérités' (*8*,
p.150). In his *Discours de la Tragédie*, published at the same time,
Corneille added yet another thought on the same topic:

> L'exclusion des personnes tout à fait vertueuses qui
> tombent dans le malheur bannit les martyrs de notre
> théâtre. Polyeucte y a réussi contre cette maxime, et
> Héraclius et Nicomède y ont plu, bien qu'ils n'impriment
> que de la pitié et ne nous donnent rien à craindre...
>
> (*2*, p.33)

Corneille's opinion therefore appears to have fluctuated somewhat as
to the exact measure of pity that a character like Nicomède was
likely to win from an audience.

Yet he never changed his mind about the principal emotion he
aimed to arouse in us with his hero, namely 'admiration'. As we saw
earlier, Corneille, when writing of Cléopâtre, intended *admirer* to
mean 'be astonished'; but it is likely that the same term applied to
Nicomède includes moral approval and even enthusiasm for his

person and his cause, as well as amazement at his 'grandeur de courage'. (*Grandeur* is also a prominent term in *Nicomède*, together with *vertu* and *générosité*, to which it is closely allied.)[17] In the *Examen* of *Nicomède*, Corneille also made large claims for 'admiration' as a substitute for the 'Aristotelian' emotions of fear and pity:

> Dans l'admiration qu'on a pour sa vertu, je trouve une manière de purger les passions dont n'a point parlé Aristote, et qui est peut-être plus sûre que celle qu'il prescrit à la tragédie par le moyen de la pitié et de la crainte. L'amour qu'elle nous donne pour cette vertu que nous admirons nous imprime de la haine pour le vice contraire. La grandeur de courage de Nicomède nous laisse une aversion de la pusillanimité... (*8*, p.150)

This important text gives us the key to Corneille's interpretation, or rather misinterpretation, of Aristotle's concept of *catharsis*. The seventeenth century tended to interpret the notion of 'purgation' or 'purification' on a moral level, that is as a reform or elimination of dangerous passions, rather than as their release or sublimation through aesthetic experience, which is the basis of the modern interpretation. To see the dire consequences of evil desires or ambitions displayed on the tragic stage was thought to be a deterrent to their gratification, and a stimulus to moral reform — this at least was the theory attributed to Aristotle by many generations of scholars. Corneille's highlighting of *admiration* in his comments on *Nicomède* underlines the exceptional importance in this play of an emotion that has been an ingredient of Cornelian tragedy ever since *Médée*. But as Scherer has observed (*22*, p.104), with *Nicomède* there comes a change of perspective. We 'admire' Rodrigue, Horace, Auguste and Polyeucte for what they accomplish in the course of the play; we can only 'admire' Nicomède, at least until the very last scene, for what he

---

[17] The most notable occurrences of the words *grand* and *grandeur* are in lines 4, 89, 320, 381, 388, 644, 819, 834, 1107, 1245, 1400, 1471, 1771, 1816. They are used ironically as well: 592-97, 933-35, 1518.

has already done. The resulting tendency towards a passive, immobile stance is reinforced by the necessity to 'keep one's hands clean', moral rectitude being a prerequisite of heroism in a confrontation that will otherwise degenerate into a naked power struggle. Corneille perhaps did well to stress the importance of 'admiration', in the case of a character who is more likely to arouse this reaction in an audience than any feelings of fraternity or affection.

It is improbable that this highly accomplished *tragédie* will convey to a twentieth-century audience much of what they will recognise as 'tragic emotion'. Modern conceptions of the tragic relate above all to the nature of the feelings aroused, and to the aesthetic experience produced by the characters and situations of a play. There must be some awareness of an impasse, of an impossible choice or an insoluble conflict. We must not, as it were, see any light at the end of the tunnel. At the end of *Nicomède*, there is a great blaze of light. All we can do in search of 'tragic quality' is to ask the question that Corneille does not invite us to ask, namely whether it is not all a mirage. Here we have a *tragédie* which satisfies all the formal criteria, and above all offers a serious, exciting and convincing political drama. But there were graver conflicts dormant in Corneille's creative imagination which were destined to surface in some of his later plays, and notably in the unadulterated tragedy of his last work, *Suréna*.

This comparative study of two outstanding seventeenth-century French tragedies has, I hope, brought to light a roughly equal number of similarities and differences between our two texts. At first, the contrasts will probably seem more remarkable than the parallels, but closer study reveals the importance of the common ground between *Rodogune* and *Nicomède*. Both are representative *tragédies* of their time, obeying all the established rules and conventions of French classical drama. Their status as tragedies can be questioned, but only by applying different aesthetic criteria, Aristotelian or modern. Both plays are dramas depicting a power-struggle in an oriental court; psychological and emotional conflict dominates in *Rodogune*, but more genuinely political problems, centred on the confrontation between monarch and hero, emerge in *Nicomède*. Each play contains a number of *romanesque* themes, but these are more important in *Rodogune* where the love element is more prominent. It is when we consider stylistic features that the contrast between the two texts becomes more apparent. *Rodogune* could be called 'high tragedy' for its stylised grandiloquence, its elaborate symmetries in construction and dialogue — all these being elements which take the play well beyond the realm of 'le vraisemblable ordinaire'. *Nicomède*, on the other hand, relies more on the cut-and-thrust of lively dialogue, on a more realistic presentation of political conflict and on a tone which is closer to the everyday or even at times to the comic than to the grandiose. The contrast is particularly marked between the final act of each play: stylised but grimly 'melodramatic', and largely on-stage, in *Rodogune*; more down-to-earth in its mostly narrated account of events, yet culminating in an almost 'fairy-tale' denouement, in *Nicomède*. The central character in each drama arouses our 'admiration', but in a different sense in each case — awe and horrified fascination as opposed to surprised enthusiasm and moral approval.

The common ground between the two works becomes apparent if we examine the basic themes they share. Both of them treat the problem of resistance to a sovereign authority that has become corrupted by the adoption of Machiavellian principles of government. The problem is different for the subjects of the ruler in question and for those who owe no such allegiance (Rodogune and Laodice). For the heir apparent in particular, the problem of rights and duties, of filial obedience weighed against legitimate self-defence, is a delicate one. To what extent in his case may injustice or violence be resisted by violent means? Both Antiochus and Nicomède are reduced to a largely passive role by the obligation to do nothing unworthy of a Christian prince or a *généreux* hero. If they fail, they may forfeit the assistance which in the end is always offered to the righteous by a benign Providence. Thus Corneille, while not concealing the ugly face of 'Machiavellian' politics, depicts it not only as evil, but also (perhaps rather optimistically) as self-defeating, or doomed because it contravenes the will of Heaven. Each play also attempts to define the nature of true kingship. *Rodogune* presents a false image of royal grandeur: Cléopâtre is attached to the outer trappings of monarchy, and to sovereign power misconstrued as the ruler's limitless *bon plaisir*. In *Nicomède*, the royal figure who becomes corrupted by evil counsels and enfeebled by submission to a foreign power, is given repeated lessons in kingship by the self-assertive heir apparent. Another important theme in both plays is the attempt to define true heroism. In particular, the notions of *vertu* and *générosité* are scrutinised. The *vertu* which in Cléopâtre's case consists solely of energy and force of character, is shown in *Nicomède* to be inseparable from respect for law and morality, and to be closely bound up with the concept of *générosité*. This is revealed in various forms in both plays: in perfect disinterestedness, in aversion to violence, in a sense of 'fair play' and above all in magnanimity in the hour of victory. Nicomède is a pure *généreux* in the chivalrous tradition, whereas Antiochus embodies a more explicitly Christian concept of heroism. Thus the characters, while not lacking in individuality, do suggest a kind of moral symbolism which transcends their purely dramatic function. We may therefore conclude that although both plays are highly successful 'dramatic machines' designed in the first place to entertain, each one was also intended by the author (with what degree of conscious purpose, it is difficult to say) to provide food for thought and themes for serious debate. But all the evidence suggests that so far as Corneille was concerned, it was 'entertainment value' that he prized above all.

# Bibliography

Of the vast and varied material published on Corneille in the last half-century, the following items are the most relevant and valuable for the study of *Rodogune* and *Nicomède*:

## EDITIONS

1. Corneille, P., *Œuvres complètes*, 3 vols, edited by G. Couton (Paris, Gallimard, Bibliothèque de la Pléiade, 1980-87). *Rodogune*: vol. II, pp.191-266 (text); pp.1268-1311 (*Notice* and notes). *Nicomède*: vol. II, pp.637-712 (text); pp.1458-96 (*Notice* and notes).
2. ——, *Writings on the Theatre*, edited by H.T. Barnwell (Oxford, Blackwell, Blackwell's French Texts, 1965).
3. ——, *Rodogune*, edited by J. Scherer (Paris, Droz, Textes Littéraires Français, 1946).
4. ——, *Rodogune*, edited by M. Cégretin (Paris, Bordas, Univers des Lettres Bordas, 1964).
5. ——, *Rodogune*, edited by P. Jolas (Paris, Larousse, Nouveaux Classiques Larousse, 1975).
6. ——, *Nicomède*, edited by R.C. Knight (London, University of London Press, Textes Français Classiques et Modernes, 1960).
7. ——, *Nicomède*, edited by E. Soufflet and M. Loiseau (Paris, Bordas, Univers des Lettres Bordas, 1964).
8. ——, *Nicomède*, edited by A. Clanet (Paris, Larousse, Nouveaux Classiques Larousse, 1975).

## BOOKS

9. Adam, A., *Histoire de la littérature française au XVIIe siècle*, 5 vols (Paris, Domat, 1948-56).
10. Barnwell, H.T., *The Tragic Drama of Corneille and Racine. An Old Parallel Revisited* (Oxford, Clarendon Press, 1982).
11. Bénichou, P., *Morales du Grand Siècle* (Paris, Gallimard, 1948).
12. Couton, G., *Corneille et la Fronde. Théâtre et politique il y a trois siècles* (Clermont-Ferrand, Bussac, 1951).

13. Couton, G., *Corneille* (Paris, Hatier, Connaissance des Lettres, 1958; 2nd edition, 1967).

14. Descotes, M., *Les Grands Rôles du théâtre de Corneille* (Paris, P.U.F., 1962).

15. Doubrovsky, S., *Corneille et la dialectique du héros* (Paris, Gallimard, 1963).

16. Goulet, A.S.-M., *L'Univers théâtral de Corneille: paradoxe et subtilité héroïques* (Cambridge, Massachusetts, Harvard University Press, 1978).

17. Harwood, S.E., *Rhetorical Techniques in Cornelian Tragedy* (Ann Arbor, University Microfilms, 1973).

18. Nadal, O., *Le Sentiment de l'amour dans l'oeuvre de Pierre Corneille* (Paris, Gallimard, 1948).

19. Nelson, R.J., *Corneille, his Heroes and their Worlds* (Philadelphia, University of Pennsylvania Press, 1963).

20. Prigent, M., *Le Héros et l'Etat dans la tragédie de Pierre Corneille* (Paris, P.U.F., 1986).

21. Scherer, J., *La Dramaturgie classique en France* (Paris, Nizet, 1959; 2nd edition, 1983).

22. ——, *Le Théâtre de Pierre Corneille* (Paris, Nizet, 1984).

23. Stegmann, A., *L'Héroïsme cornélien, genèse et signification*, 2 vols (Paris, Colin, 1968).

24. Sweetser M.-O., *La Dramaturgie de Corneille* (Geneva, Droz, 1977).

25. Voltaire, *Commentaires sur Corneille*, edited by David Williams, in *Complete Works*, vols 52-54 (Banbury, Voltaire Foundation, 1974).

26. Yarrow, P.J., *Corneille* (London, Macmillan, 1963).

*ARTICLES*

27. Descotes, M., 'L'Image de Rome dans *La Mort de Pompée* et *Nicomède*', *Romanistische Zeitschrift für Literaturgeschischte*, 3 (1979), 31-75.

28. Dosmond, S., 'La Rome de Corneille', *L'Information littéraire*, 36, 4 (1984), 142-52.

29. Fromilhague, R., 'A propos de la Cléopâtre de *Rodogune*', *Cahiers de littérature du XVIIe siècle*, 1 (1979), 43-53.

30. Fumaroli, M., 'Tragique païen et tragique chrétien dans *Rodogune*', *Revue des sciences humaines*, 38 (1973), 599-631.

31. Georges, A., 'Le Personnage de Rodogune dans *Rodogune, princesse des Parthes* de Pierre Corneille', *Les Lettres romanes*, 35, 1-2 (1981), 91-127.

32. ——, 'Nicomède ou le magnanime aristotélicien', *Revue de l'histoire du théâtre*, 36 (1984), 153-79.

33. Gossip, C., 'The Problem of *Rodogune*', *Studi Francesi*, 22 (1978), 231-40.

34. Griffiths, B., '"La fourbe" and "la générosité": fair and foul play in *Nicomède*', *Forum for Modern Language Studies*, 1 (1965), 339-57.

35. Herland, L., Reply to articles on *Rodogune* by R. Jasinski, *Revue d'histoire littéraire de la France*, 51 (1951), 126-28.

36. Jasinski, R., 'Psychologie de Rodogune', *Revue d'histoire littéraire de la France*, 49 (1949), 209-19, 322-38.

37. ——, 'Le Sens de *Rodogune*' in *Mélanges d'histoire littéraire offerts à Monsieur Daniel Mornet* (Paris, Nizet, 1951), pp.63-71.

38. ——, 'Sur *Nicomède*' in *A travers le XVIIe siècle*, 2 vols (Paris, Nizet, 1981), I, pp.118-35 (also reprints the two articles on *Rodogune*, I, pp.76-117).

39. Knight, R.C., 'Corneille, *Pompée* to *Pertharite*', *Seventeenth-Century French Studies*, 7 (1985), 17-26.

40. ——, '*Cosroès* and *Nicomède*' in *The French Mind. Studies in Honour of Gustave Rudler*, edited by W.G. Moore, R. Sutherland and E. Starkie (Oxford, Clarendon Press, 1952), pp.54-69.

41. Mourgues, O.de, '*Rodogune*, tragédie de la Renaissance' in *Pierre Corneille: actes du colloque de Rouen, 1984* (Paris, P.U.F., 1985), pp.483-88.

42. Pich, E., '*Nicomède*, les comédiens et le public' in *Actes du colloque de Tunis* (Paris, Seattle, Tübingen, PFSCL, Biblio 17, no. 26, 1986), pp.77-103.

43. Scherer, J., 'Les Intentions politiques dans *Nicomède*' in *Pierre Corneille: actes du colloque de Rouen, 1984* (Paris, P.U.F., 1985), pp.493-99.

44. Vier, J., 'Réflexions sur *Rodogune*' in *Littérature à l'emporte-pièce*, I (Paris, Du Cèdre, 1958), pp.3-11.

# CRITICAL GUIDES TO FRENCH TEXTS

*edited by*
Roger Little, Wolfgang van Emden, David Williams

1. **David Bellos.** Balzac: La Cousine Bette.
2. **Rosemarie Jones.** Camus: L'Etranger *and* La Chute.
3. **W.D Redfern.** Queneau: Zazie dans le métro.
4. **R.C. Knight.** Corneille: Horace.
5. **Christopher Todd.** Voltaire: Dictionnaire philosophique.
6. **J.P. Little.** Beckett: En attendant Godot *and* Fin de partie.
7. **Donald Adamson.** Balzac: Illusions perdues.
8. **David Coward.** Duras: Moderato cantabile.
9. **Michael Tilby.** Gide: Les Faux-Monnayeurs.
10. **Vivienne Mylne.** Diderot: La Religieuse.
11. **Elizabeth Fallaize.** Malraux: La Voie Royale.
12. **H.T Barnwell.** Molière: Le Malade imaginaire.
13. **Graham E. Rodmell.** Marivaux: Le Jeu de l'amour et du hasard *and* Les Fausses Confidences.
14. **Keith Wren.** Hugo: Hernani *and* Ruy Blas.
15. **Peter S. Noble.** Beroul's Tristan *and the* Folie de Berne.
16. **Paula Clifford.** Marie de France: Lais.
17. **David Coward.** Marivaux: La Vie de Marianne *and* Le Paysan parvenu.
18. **J.H. Broome.** Molière: L'Ecole des femmes *and* Le Misanthrope.
19. **B.G. Garnham.** Robbe-Grillet: Les Gommes *and* Le Voyeur.
20. **J.P. Short.** Racine: Phèdre.
21. **Robert Niklaus.** Beaumarchais: Le Mariage de Figaro.
22. **Anthony Cheal Pugh.** Simon: Histoire.
23. **Lucie Polak.** Chrétien de Troyes: Cligés.
24. **John Cruickshank.** Pascal: Pensées.
25. **Ceri Crossley.** Musset: Lorenzaccio.
26. **J.W Scott.** Madame de Lafayette: La Princesse de Clèves.
27. **John Holyoake**. Montaigne: Essais.
28. **Peter Jimack.** Rousseau: Emile.
29. **Roger Little.** Rimbaud: Illuminations.